Country Decorating

TIME-LIFE BOOKS

Alexandria, Virginia

Country Decorating

*creative ways
to bring country style
into your home*

A R E B U S B O O K

CONTENTS

stenciling. A chapter on fabrics looks at traditional styles for curtains, bedcoverings and canopies, and furniture upholstery. And a chapter on accessories shows how details can make a big difference in the appearance of a room: there are ideas for lighting fixtures and hardware, as well as original ways to highlight mantelpieces, desk tops, and even staircases with collectibles.

While a familiarity with these elements will help make any decorating scheme successful, the country look evoked on the following pages involves something more: a sense of the history that is intrinsic to what we now think of as country. In furnishing their homes, America's settlers made inventive, thrifty use of whatever materials they had on hand, combining local craft traditions and ethnic customs to produce a decorative heritage that is in many ways unique to this nation. The paint treatments they applied to walls and floors, such as murals and stencils, and the homemade floor coverings they made from hooked, braided, or woven fabric scraps, developed from a desire to have beauty, warmth, and color in the home at a time when luxuries were scarce.

Today, the look of country style relies on that same spirit of ingenuity and spontaneity, and it is that legacy that sets American country apart from all other approaches to decorating.

The Elements of Decorating

the basic principles of interior design

Although decorating in the country style permits an informal, unstructured approach, it still requires an understanding of the basic elements of good interior design—among them color, pattern, and texture. Color plays a significant role in decorating, not only because it is so easy for people to respond to, but because it can also be used to unify the furnishings in a room and to set an overall tone. Your color preferences will ultimately affect your choice of furniture, fabrics, and accessories.

Pattern and texture are equally important decorating considerations. Whether you choose one motif—a star or checkerboard, perhaps—or use a combination, pattern can give a decor focus and visual interest. Texture—be it in a stone wall surface, a hand-hewn wood floor, or a curtain made from antique lace—adds further dimension to a room and can affect the way both color and pattern are perceived. As you will see on the following pages, all three elements may be combined in any number of ways to achieve a successful country look.

Traditional colors and patterns distinguish the decor of a country dining room.

Traditional Color

Of all the elements in decorating, color is among the most useful. Not only can it have a strong visual impact, but it can also set a mood, or recall a historical period.

To evoke an early American look, the owners of this midwestern farmhouse painted their parlor with varied shades of muted green, a color that had become popular by the second half of the 18th century. By choosing a darker hue for the fireplace and wall paneling, above, and the wainscoting and trim, right, they called atten-

tion to the handsome woodwork. These features are further set off by the tint of yellow green and the stenciled border on the walls and fireboard.

The upholstered furniture also coordinates with the period color scheme. The green plaid fabric on the wing chair is a reproduction of an 18th-century pattern. For contrast, the Chippendale-style camelback sofa was covered in a navy tone-on-tone flame-stitch pattern; its deep blue recalls the color of indigo, a dye widely used in fabrics during America's early years.

To arrive at a traditional shade of muted green for the pine paneling, above, and the wainscoting and

trim, right, the owners of this farmhouse applied a green glaze over a base coat of blue paint.

Contrasting Colors

In the bedroom at right, the neutral white of the walls and ceiling prevent the contrast of red and blue from becoming overpowering.

Using two contrasting hues, which appear to intensify when they are placed side by side, is a particularly good way to create a dramatic color scheme. In the bedroom at left, for example, the strong red of the settee upholstery is picked up in the quilts, rug, and wall hanging, creating a striking effect against the blue color of the woodwork.

An equally vivid contrast was achieved when the entry hall above was painted red, separating the space visually from the adjoining parlor, where the paneling is blue. The oriental rug picks up both colors.

Because red and blue, used in the entry hall and the parlor of the 1790s house above, are strong colors, the homeowner kept the rest of the decor understated. The pine-plank floors were left unpainted; simple furnishings include a bow-back Windsor chair.

Neutral Backdrops

T his living room and entry hall illustrate one of the most versatile of all color schemes: neutrals enlivened with bright accents. Here soft variations of white—compatible with any hue—create a basic background; against it, colorful accessories and painted details are particularly noticeable.

In the living room, left, the neutral decor shows off the bright rag rug and other colorful touches to advantage. Picking up the colors of the rug, the quilt and sofa pillows become strong accents against the off-white seating upholstery patterned with a subtle herringbone. In the adjacent hall, above, other neutrals—ivory-colored walls and dark oak woodwork—set off the hand-painted trompe l'oeil "tiles" on the wall borders and staircase.

By adding hand-painted decoration, the owners of this Long Island country house turned a nondescript hall into a welcoming entryway. A marine varnish finish was applied to the decoration for protection.

Off-white makes an effective backdrop for the colorful rug and pillows in the living room at left.

Understanding Color

Beyond being merely pleasing to the eye, color can work hard in a room. With color, you can evoke a certain atmosphere, achieve a feeling of warmth or coolness, alter the perception of space and dimension, or simply provide visual interest where there is none.

cool colors

Infinite in their possibilities, the relationships of colors—also known as hues—are quite complicated. To understand them, color theorists usually think of the color spectrum as a wheel divided into three color types—primary, secondary, and tertiary—located at equidistant intervals.

The primary colors are red, blue, and yellow. These are the only pure colors in the spectrum, meaning they cannot be produced by mixing any other colors. When two primary colors are blended in equal parts, they form the secondary hues: violet, green, and orange. The six tertiary colors—blue violet, blue green, yellow green, yellow orange, red orange, and red violet—are created when a primary color is mixed with an adjacent secondary hue.

One half of the color wheel includes the violets, blues, and greens, which are known as cool colors. Considered refreshing and restful, cool colors are a good choice for a room in which you want to create a soothing effect, or for a hot, sunny space that you wish to "cool down."

The other half of the color wheel comprises the yellows, oranges, and reds, which are known as warm colors. Warm hues are thought of as "active," and they generally create a cheerful appearance.

Neutrals—black, white, gray, brown, and beige—are not found in the spectrum or on the color wheel and technically are not colors. Their impact on color, however, makes them important factors in any decorating scheme. Because neutrals are neither warm nor cool, they can be used to help unify a mix of colors in a single room, to create an effective backdrop for bright colors, or to offer relief from intense color. Pale gray walls, for example, will help neutralize the color scheme in a room where vibrant hues, such as bright blues, dominate in the carpeting and upholstery.

Understanding color value and saturation is also important in achieving a successful combination of colors. Value is the degree of light and dark in a color. A red mixed with white to form pastel pink is high in value; a red darkened with black to form maroon is low in value. Saturation refers to the intensity, or brilliance, of a color. A clear red is highly saturated with red pigment, whereas a red that has been mixed with another color is low in saturation.

Painting the walls and ceiling of a room a highly saturated or a dark color—a deep green, perhaps—will make it seem smaller. Using a color

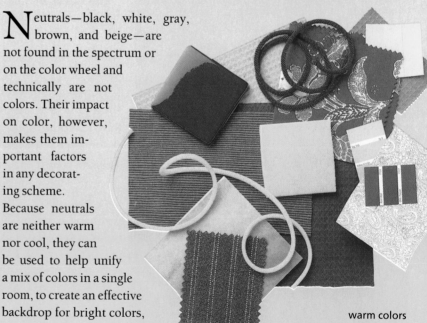

warm colors

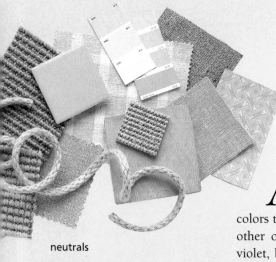

neutrals

wheel. Triads—yellow, red, and blue, for example—generally depend on subtle shadings of the colors to be effective.

Analogous, or related, schemes are based on colors that are adjacent to one another on the wheel—such as violet, blue violet, and red violet—and they are considered to be particularly harmonious combinations.

In a monochromatic scheme, one color in a range of values and intensities is used with a neutral, such as black or white. A simple monochromatic scheme would comprise one basic color, one tint (the color mixed with white), and one shade (the color

they do demand diversity in texture and pattern, as well as care in matching and combining colors to keep the scheme from becoming monotonous. The gradated hues on paint-color samples, which are available at paint

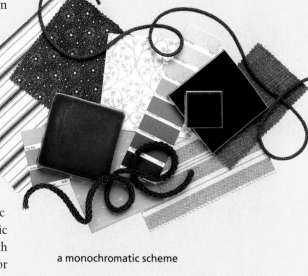

a monochromatic scheme

high in value—such as pale blue—will make the room seem larger.

Value and saturation can also be used to highlight or disguise details or objects in a room. You might draw attention to fine woodwork by painting it a dark color, and the surrounding walls a lighter shade. Or, you can play down an unattractive piece of furniture by putting it against a background that has a color similar in value and saturation so that it blends in unobtrusively.

Most home decorating schemes are based on the relationship of colors on the color wheel as well as on value and saturation. In complementary schemes, for instance, colors that are opposite each other on the color wheel—red and green, yellow and violet, orange and blue—are paired together to create vibrant contrasts. In most complementary schemes one color is dominant and the other is used as an accent.

Triadic schemes are created by combining any three colors that are equidistant from one another on the

low-value colors

mixed with black). A monochromatic scheme of green, for example, might incorporate a bright kelly green, a pastel green, and a dark forest green.

While monochromatic schemes are among the simplest to devise,

stores, will help you select a variety of values that blend together well.

To be effective, any color scheme should follow some general rules of thumb. A room in which color dominates, for example, can seem disjointed if there is too much contrast; but hues of similar values, such as pastels, will always harmonize even if they include both warm and cool colors.

When you are using three or more colors in the same room, it is wise to pick one that will dominate the walls, then introduce others that are closely matched in value. The scheme will still leave room for an occasional bright- or dark-colored accessory.

Thematic Patterns

Pattern is another fundamental element in decorating. In addition to appearing in fabrics, rugs, and wallcoverings, patterns can also be formed by the shapes and groupings of furniture, by paintings on a wall, by a display of collectibles, by the play of light and shade. In general, the key to combining patterns effectively is to relate them through scale, color, proportion, or, as in the two rooms shown here, by theme.

In the bedroom above, two strong patterns— in the 19th-century quilt and on the painted floor—are unified by their stylized star motifs. "We wanted a relaxed feeling, so we told the artist to have a good time," says the owner. "The floor just evolved."

The patterns in the log cabin living room at right were inspired by the geometric lines of the structure itself. The sofa upholstery is adapted from a traditional Log Cabin quilt pattern, which here features light and dark strips that suggest the look of chinked log walls. The striped pillow and the twig floor lamp add their own strong lines to the room.

In the bedroom above and the log cabin living room at right, combinations of bold thematic motifs make strong decorating statements.

Graphic Patterns

The bold colors and distinctive silhouettes of graphic patterns dominate these two country-style bedrooms. For a traditional look, the owner of the 18th-century house opposite based the decor of her master bedroom on a striking mix of stars, checks, and diamonds. The floor features a large-scale painted checkerboard; picking up its salmon and green color scheme, the antique hooked rugs play off the grid with their lozenge designs.

Smaller diamonds appear in the hooked hearth rug mounted on the wall, while the Stars in Grids quilt adds its own distinctive pattern to the colorful composition.

The room above also displays an imaginative interplay of patterns. The stenciled wall design was inspired by an original painted by the 19th-century itinerant artist Moses Eaton, Jr. The mid-19th-century wool and linen blanket and the cut lampshade were chosen to coordinate with the painted patterns.

In the bedroom above, oval boxes (painted by the homeowner), a flower-painted traveling trunk, and an 18th-century flame-stitch sand weight—used to hold books open—add a range of colorful patterns to the space.

Pinks, greens, and beiges help unify the bold patterns of the quilt, late-19th-century hooked rugs, and custom-painted floor in the bedroom opposite.

Garden Patterns

T he owners of this country retreat chose patterns inspired by its rural setting to express a relaxed mood in their living room, left and above. The room is enlivened by the bold floral-stripe fabric used for the draperies, sofa upholstery, balloon shade, and window seat with matching pillow. Botanical prints and other accessories, including the flowered needlepoint pillow cover and the hooked rug decorated with leaves and tendrils above, emphasize the garden theme.

Floor-to-ceiling draperies, above, create the illusion of more height in the living room. A beribboned lampshade adds a romantic touch.

Wicker chairs and sea grass matting bring a gardenlike feeling to this cottage living room.

MIXING AND MATCHING

The variety of wallcovering and fabric patterns available today offers countless possibilities for decorating, but choosing among these patterns doesn't have to be a daunting experience. To make the task easier, many manufacturers offer collections of wallpapers and fabrics specially designed to go together. You can also select each individually or mix patterns from different manufacturers. It helps to shop for wallcoverings and fabrics at the same store, but if you are choosing them at different stores, bring along large swatches of the patterns you are considering; never try to recall patterns and colors from memory.

Before choosing wallpaper or fabric patterns, first settle on a color scheme. Keep in mind how the room will be used, as well as the mood you want to create. And be sure to select a color you particularly like—surprisingly, many people don't do this, and they end up regretting their choice. Inspiration may come from a favorite rug, a piece of furniture, even a painting.

After you have decided on a color scheme, you may want to think about a unifying theme for the wallpaper and fabric patterns. One possibility is to stick with a particular motif, such as a floral or a plaid. Your theme can also be a look: a traditional feeling, for example, might be achieved with a mix of small checks, stars, and stripes. Textured neutrals, on the other hand, can produce a subtle, sophisticated look.

With your colors and themes in mind, you should next consider the scale of the patterns. It is generally best to pick patterns that differ in scale—some large, some small—because patterns of the same size will appear to "fight."

It is also a good idea to vary the frequency with which patterns appear. Use some patterns lavishly and others sparingly; this will add variety and interest to a room. One simple strategy is to cover larger expanses, such as walls or sofas, with a large-scale print, and to choose a mini-print design in a related color for smaller wall areas, curtains, pillows, or chairs. You can accent a room with well-placed punches of color—on pillows or lampshades, perhaps. Incorporating a few subdued patterns or solids into your scheme will keep the decor from becoming overpowering.

At right are some examples of how patterned wallpapers and fabrics can be effectively combined. Each scheme incorporates a chair rail, which can be used as an accent, serve as a transition between two wall treatments, or hide wallpaper seams. These wallpapers and fabrics are all coordinated with an eye to color, theme, and scale. See page 170 for additional information.

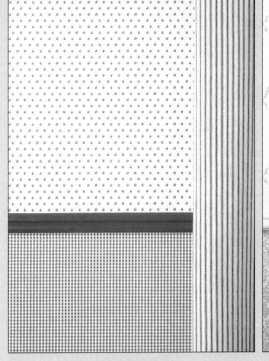

All-American: Unified by a blue chair rail, calico- and gingham-print wallcoverings mix well with ticking fabric.

Coordinated florals: A cheerful flower motif relates two wallcoverings. Checked fabric picks up touches of blue.

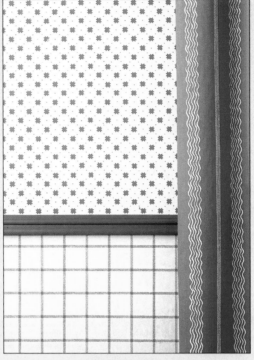

astels: Flower-sprigged fabric sets a
astel color scheme for two wallcover-
ngs related by a subtle diamond grid.

Stripes and fruits: Striped wallpaper
picks up the lines of the wainscoting;
the peach fabric is color-coordinated.

Colonial: A rust color scheme unifies
colonial motifs: redware sgraffito
squiggles, homespun plaid, tiny stars.

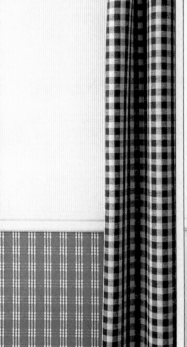

Traditional patterns: Red, white, and
blue stripes and plaids recall the patterns of homespun.

Neutrals: Tone-on-tone wallpapers
in beige, and a subtly textured fabric,
create a soft, restful feeling.

Paisley and foulard: A sophisticated
English country look comes from deep-
colored patterns.

Rustic Textures

Texture also plays an important role in decorating. Textured surfaces, whether rough or smooth, not only add their own feeling to a room, but affect the way color and pattern are perceived.

In the 19th-century cabin kitchen at left and above, the rustic look comes primarily from the rough materials of the house itself: log walls, plastered fireplace, and brick hearth. Simple painted furniture, and accessories such as dried herbs, baskets, and nubby homespun curtains, enhance the primitive feeling.

Above, accessories, including a southern-made basket and a blue-painted spice box, complement the rustic surroundings.

A worn red-painted table, left, adds color as well as texture to this country kitchen.

A Mix of Textures

The mottled texture of the stone wall above, which was not refinished when this 1760s barn was remodeled, creates a dramatic contrast with the smooth surfaces of the mirror, Georgian-period English candelabra, and inlaid Federal-style chest.

Contrasting textures give a surprisingly sophisticated look to this renovated 18th-century barn, where walls of field-stone and aging stucco create a rough back-drop for a collection of heirloom furniture.

In the bedroom, right, the texture and ran-dom pattern of the walls are emphasized by the soft carpeting and the fine lines of the ma-hogany bed. The unusual juxtaposition contin-ues on the stair landing, above, where a bow-front chest, silver candelabra, and gilt-frame mirror stand out against the pitted wall surface.

A crocheted spread and lacy pillows provide soft touches in the stone-walled bedroom at right.

Elegant Textures

The delicate textures of linen and lace give an elegant, romantic feeling to this living room in a city apartment. By using lavishly draped curtains, luxurious pillows, and a dhurrie rug, the owners softened the rough look of the brick walls and added visual interest to the space.

The floor-to-ceiling windows, covered in embroidered cutwork linen with a subtly textured pattern, are the focal point of the room. The graceful drapery blocks an unappealing view, yet admits enough sunshine to brighten the room and to create a subtle play of shadows.

At left, a pine day bed is invitingly heaped with lace-covered pillows, and a lace runner tempers the modern look of the coffee table. The 19th-century silver tea service, above, which includes both French and Italian pieces, adds its own smooth texture to the mix.

On the settee above, polished silver and a straw basket filled with tulips complement the starched linens.

In this city living room, soft draperies, romantic lace, and delicate linens, left, were chosen to play off the rough texture of the brick walls.

Glossary of Decorating Terms

ARCHITECTURAL TERMS

◆*baseboard* A horizontal molding, usually flat, running along the base of a wall at floor level.

◆*beam* A horizontal structural member that helps support a floor or ceiling.

◆*column* A round, freestanding pillar consisting of a capital, or top, a shaft, and a base.

◆*chair rail* A horizontal molding running along a wall about three feet above floor level. Originally used to prevent a wall surface from being damaged by chair backs; now often purely decorative.

◆*cornice* A horizontal band of ornamental molding that runs along the top of a wall at ceiling level.

◆*dado* See wainscot.

◆*molding* A decorative band—usually of wood or plaster—used to conceal structural joints or to introduce dimension to a wall surface.

◆*pilaster* A nonstructural architectural element that has a base, a top, or capital, and the general appearance of a column, but is usually rectangular, rather than round, in form. Unlike a column, which is freestanding, a pilaster projects slightly from a wall.

◆*tongue and groove* A joint in which a tongue, or projection, on one edge of a board fits into a corresponding groove, or channel, on the edge of another board.

◆*trim* The moldings used to frame doors and windows.

◆*wainscot* A decorative treatment—often paneling—used to finish the lower part of an interior wall. Also known as dado.

WINDOW TREATMENT TERMS

◆*austrian blind* A shirred fabric blind made with vertical rows of stitching pulled up into gathers.

◆*balloon blind* A fabric blind with deep, inverted folds that create a billowy effect when the blind is raised.

◆*blind* A flexible screen, usually of fabric or paper, that can be raised, lowered, or otherwise moved to regulate light. Also known as a shade. See also venetian blind.

◆*cafe curtain* A straight-hanging curtain used to cover the bottom half of a window. Usually hung in pairs from a rod by loops or rings.

◆*drapery* A curtain of heavy fabric, sometimes used over a sheer undercurtain. Usually hung in pairs.

◆*festoon curtain* A simple, straight panel fitted on the back with rings through which a cord is passed to gather the fabric into a swag.

◆*heading* The top part of a curtain extending above the rod.

◆*roman shade* A shade that draws up into neat horizontal pleats when it is raised.

◆*shade* See blind.

◆*swag curtain* A curtain in which a single horizontal length of fabric is caught near its ends so that the middle section of the fabric falls in a graceful curve over the window.

◆*tieback* A fastener, usually made of ribbon, fabric, or braid, that is attached to the sides of the window and holds back draperies or curtains.

◆*valance* A short curtain or panel of fabric, or a slightly projecting horizontal box, that is placed at the top of a curtain or drapery to conceal the hanging hardware, such as rod and rings, or the heading.

◆*venetian blind* A shade made of horizontal slats—usually of wood or metal—that are strung one above the other at even intervals and can be angled simultaneously to regulate light.

UPHOLSTERY TERMS

◆*piping* A narrow fabric edging or cording used to trim pillows and upholstery.

◆*railroading* A method used in upholstering or slipcovering by which a fabric with a vertically striped pattern is used horizontally.

◆*repeat* The distance between repeating motifs on a fabric.

◆*shirring* A method for gathering fabric in which three or more parallel lines of stitching are pulled to draw the fabric gently together.

◆*slipcover* A fitted, removable covering for a piece of seating furniture, which is generally upholstered.

◆*tassel* A bunch of threads, bound at one end and free at the other, used as a decorative trimming.

◆*upholstery* The springs, stuffing, cushions, and fabric used to make a soft covering for furniture.

◆*welting* A tape or covered cord that is sewn into a seam for decoration or reinforcement.

PAINT TREATMENTS

◆*antiquing* A process in which a paint, varnish, or glaze is applied to a surface and then blotted off with a cloth while still damp to suggest the appearance of age.

◆*combing* A process in which a comb —often made of heavy cardboard— is pulled across wet paint on a surface to create a striped, often wavy pattern.

◆*dragging* A process in which a dry paintbrush is dragged through a wet glaze on a surface to create a subtle pattern of fine lines.

◆*glazing* A process in which a film of oil-base color is applied to a painted surface to create a semitransparent effect.

◆*graining* A process in which one or more tools, such as feathers or sticks, are dragged through a wet glaze to suggest the effect of wood graining.

◆*marbling* A process in which colors are blended and streaked—usually with a brush or sponge—and often veined to suggest the appearance of marble.

◆*pickling* A process in which a white or light paint is applied to a wooden surface, then partially wiped off with a soft cloth while still damp to reveal the natural grain of the wood underneath.

◆*ragging* A process in which a wet glaze or paint is dabbed on or blotted off a surface with a rag or paper towels to produce a textured effect.

◆*spattering* A process in which thinned paint is splashed in small drops onto a surface, usually with a paintbrush.

◆*sponging* A process in which a glaze or paint is dabbed on or blotted off a surface with a sponge for a soft, textured effect.

◆*stenciling* A process in which paint is dabbed with a brush or sponge—or sprayed—onto a surface through a cut-out pattern.

◆*stippling* A process in which the tip of a dry brush is dabbed firmly onto a wet glaze or paint to produce a soft, matte finish.

◆*trompe l'oeil painting* A process in which a flat image is rendered in paint so as to appear three-dimensional, deceiving the eye.

Cozy Groupings

Furniture arrangement not only affects the look of a room, but can also reflect its function. To encourage relaxation and conversation, the furniture in the large seaside living room above, for example, was separated into two smaller groupings that are unified by color and pattern: gray and white chintz for the chairs and ottoman, flowered chintz for the sofas.

Defined by symmetrical arrangements, the seating areas were situated near the room's natural focal points: the fireplace and a bay

In the Maine living room at left, color and pattern were used to link two separate seating areas, as well as to create a summery look for the entire space. To enhance the casual spirit of the room, the homeowner added outdoor touches, including wicker chairs, an Adirondack-style twig table, and a mirror in a twiglike frame.

window overlooking the ocean. At the hearth, two armchairs share an ottoman; tied together by the area rug, this grouping is completed by the nearby sofa. The painted bench serves as a coffee table and its narrow shape leaves ample space for people to pass by easily.

In the seating area at the window, wicker chairs keep the setting light and airy and can be turned readily to take advantage of the view. The simple green coffee table was custom-made to fit the space and to complement the casual look of the room.

Shaker Unity

The simple decor of the dining room at right focuses on a collection of 19th-century Shaker furniture. Shaker pieces tend to have a uniform look because woodworking was a communal enterprise among these people. Like all their handwork, Shaker furniture embodies the religious sect's tenets of neatness, order, and simplicity.

One effective way to decorate a room is to take a deliberately cohesive approach. This dining room draws its unified look from a collection of 19th-century Shaker pieces, which the owners admire for their simplicity and fine craftsmanship.

Dominating the room is the eleven-foot-long trestle table at left, typical of the tables that once accommodated the Shakers at their communal meals. Around it are two sets of ladder-back chairs, one with cloth-tape seats and the other with cane seats. Two case pieces—a squat chest, or tailoring bunk, and a tall cupboard over drawers—provide storage. Above, Shaker-made hangers and boxes keep the look consistent.

To lighten the stark look of their Shaker-style dining room, the homeowners added a whimsical rocking horse, above, and a portrait by Ammi Phillips, a 19th-century American folk painter.

Eclectic Decorating

Situated at one side of the living room, the carved chest above has been draped with an old shawl that plays off the colors of the framed map on the wall.

An eclectic decor can be just as successful as one that is unified. When furnishing this living room, the homeowners explored auctions and tag sales looking for comfortable pieces that would blend well with their vintage shawls, coverlets, and prints. Found at a local flea market, old draperies, for example, were recycled into the new set of curtains and the matching balloon shade, right. The varied fabric patterns in the room are harmonized by the rich, red-dominated color scheme, picked up in the fringed shawl, above.

A casual mix of furniture and fabrics, right, gives a cozy feeling to this living room.

Walls and Ceilings

imaginative ways to give these
"backdrop" surfaces a variety
of country looks

While walls, and sometimes ceilings, generally serve as a background for the furnishings in a room, they can also make an important contribution to its overall appearance and character. When planning a country decorating scheme, keep in mind the many treatments possible for walls and ceilings: they often define a particular look even before the furniture and accessories are added.

For early Americans, painting was one of the least expensive and most versatile ways to bring color into the home. Today, many homeowners continue to use traditional painted decorations, such as stencil designs and murals. Architectural features—exposed beams and wood paneling, for example—can also add character to a room or create a period feeling. Or try experimenting with wallpaper: available in a wide range of contemporary and historical patterns, it can be used just as effectively on ceilings as on walls.

A delicate stenciled border adds detail to a paneled wall.

Dramatic Walls

One of the simplest ways to make walls an effective decorating element in a room is to paint them a striking color. Inspired by her views of the Atlantic Ocean, the owner of this island summer home chose a seawater blue for the walls of her library, and lighter tints for the doors and trim. Rather than overwhelming the artwork and furnishings—including the 1854 needlepoint sampler over the mantel, left, and the sea chest above—the prominent background color enhances their beauty.

A solid expanse of blue dominates the library at left, creating a restful look.

With its colorful nautical painting, the antique sea chest above is at home in the oceanside room.

Painted Paneling

Flowered chintz curtains pick up the dusty rose color of the beaded-board walls in the bedroom above. The walnut bed dates from around 1850.

The owners of this 1890 Gothic farmhouse near New Orleans spent over a year renovating the building before they moved in. Among the pleasant discoveries awaiting them was the original beaded-board pine paneling, uncovered when the modern gypsum wallboard and false ceilings were torn away.

Such machine-made paneling, a product of America's Industrial Revolution, was particularly popular during the Victorian era. Because its simple look suited their country decor, the homeowners left the woodwork in place, rejuvenating it with paint—pink in the bedroom, above, and green in the living room, opposite.

Remodeled with built-in bookshelves and cushioned window seats, a window bay becomes a focal point of the living room opposite.

A Primer on Paints

Today, we think nothing of heading to the nearest paint or hardware store when it is time to redecorate, but until mass-produced paints first became widely available in the 1800s, painting meant mixing the materials from scratch.

The process was not only time-consuming, but laborious. In his 1812 treatise *Directions for House and Ship Painting*, Hezekiah Reynolds, a Connecticut painter, suggested the following recipe for preparing a basic oil paint for interior work:

"Use a brass or copper kettle—cover the bottom of the vessel with red lead . . . in the proportion of half a pound to each gallon of oil; boil the same over a slow fire, untill [sic] the oil will singe a feather; then let it cool, and add one gill of Copal Varnish, or Spirits of Turpentine to each gallon of oil." While it is no longer necessary to cook up such concoctions yourself, buying paint at a store can pose its own challenges, unless you are familiar with the materials and know what equipment is required.

When you buy paint for interiors, choosing the color will be among your first considerations. Most stores offer color samples, called paint chips, to their customers free of charge; after you have selected a few, take them outdoors to compare the colors in natural light. Better still, take the samples home before you make your final decision so that you can see how they look in the room you are planning to paint; be sure to check their appearance under daytime and nighttime lighting conditions. The color will appear slightly stronger on the wall than on the paint chip.

While some paints are available in stock colors, any color you choose from a paint chip needs to be custom-mixed in the store while you wait. When you do buy custom-mixed paint, it is a good idea to purchase all of the paint that you need at the same time; if you go back for more later, the color could differ slightly from your original batch. If you buy more than one can of the same color, mix your paint using some from each can so that the color remains consistent. As a rule, you will need a gallon of paint for every 300 to 400 square feet to be covered. Unless you are painting over a similar color, you should plan on applying two coats.

Once you have selected a paint color, you will need to keep in mind that specific interior paints are sold for specific surfaces—floors, ceilings, walls—so be sure you are buying the right paint for your purpose. There are two basic kinds of interior paint: primer and finish paint. Primer, which is usually white but can be tinted to approximate the color of your final coat, is used to prepare a surface—especially new or unpainted wallboard, plaster, or wood—so that it will bond well to the finish paint. Special primers are also available to cover stains and knotholes that may show through paint. The finish paint is the paint you will use for the final coats.

Most primers and finish paints come in two basic types: alkyd and latex. Alkyd, also known as oil-base paint, is a solvent-thinned paint that takes about 24 hours to dry and requires paint thinner or turpentine for cleanup. Alkyd paint produces a smooth, durable, water-resistant surface, and is recommended for use in rooms where walls might need frequent cleaning, such as in a kitchen, or where they are exposed to moisture, as in a bathroom.

Latex, generally less expensive than alkyd paint, is a water-thinned paint that produces a slightly rougher surface than alkyd paint. It dries in a few hours and requires only soap and water for cleanup. Latex is fine for window and door trim and walls in rooms that do not need a lot of cleaning. As a rule, alkyd paint can be used over alkyd or latex paint, but latex paint bonds well only to other latex paints.

Both alkyd and latex paints are available in several different finishes; the three most basic are flat, semigloss, and high-gloss. Flat paint produces a porous, soft-looking surface. Of the three finishes, it is the least resistant to abrasion, and tends to absorb moisture and grease; it is not recommended for kitchens and bathrooms.

Semigloss paint dries with a hard surface and a slight sheen that does not show scuffs or smudges as readily as flat paint. Because it is easy to wipe clean, semigloss is a good choice for kitch- ens, chil- dren's rooms, and woodwork. It also reflects light, which can make a room seem brighter.

High-gloss paint, which is the most durable, dries with a very bright sheen and produces a tough surface that stands up to frequent cleaning. Its use is generally limited to cabinets and woodwork in kitchens and bathrooms.

After choosing your paint, you will also need to consider equipment. Most people prefer a roller for large areas and use brushes for corners, edging, and woodwork. The most common roller sizes are 7- and 9-inch lengths; novice painters will probably find the smaller size easier to work with. Choose one with a sturdy handle, and be sure to buy the right size pan for the width of the roller. Roller covers, which can be purchased separately, are availa- ble with different naps. The thicker naps are meant for use on rough-tex- tured walls, but because they are likely to spatter the paint, they can be messy to work with. On most surfaces, a short-nap roller will give the clean- est, smoothest paint finish.

When purchasing brushes, look for those with dense bristles that spring back into shape when you bounce them against your hand. Brushes with natural bristles are recommended for use with alkyd paints, while nylon bristles are good for latex. All brushes should have flagged (split) ends that help spread paint evenly.

Use the largest brush possible for each job; a large brush will hold more paint and produce a smoother application than a smaller one. A 2-inch, angle-cut sash brush is suitable for window frames, a 3½- or 4-inch brush is good for cupboards and doors. For walls, choose a 5-inch brush with 4- or 5-inch-long bristles. Be sure to clean and dry your brushes thoroughly im- mediately after use.

The best way to ensure a professional-looking paint job is to follow the directions on the products you use. Keep your work area well ven- tilated, especially when using al- kyd paint. Let gravity help you avoid drips on completed work: start by painting the ceiling, then move on to the walls next, and end with the woodwork. And be sure to leave yourself time to do the job right.

Versatile Wallpaper

Wallpaper not only makes a pretty addition to a country room, but it also serves as a useful problem-solver. By wallpapering, you can unify a decor or bring interest to an otherwise dull room. Wallpaper also camouflages uneven plaster or an old paint job. And it can have a significant effect on the mood of a room. Indeed, it is the wallpaper that enhances the atmosphere in these two bedrooms tucked up under sloping roofs.

The bedroom above, in a guest house on a Pennsylvania farm, gains its snug, cozy feeling from a strawberry-print paper used to cover the ceiling as well as the walls. By painting the trim and rafters white and adding ruffled curtains, the homeowners kept the look simple and homey. Auctions and flea markets yielded the old iron bed, antique white coverlet, and washbasin and pitcher.

The bedroom at right is in a Victorian farmhouse in California, built in 1876. Although the exposed rafters and roofing give this attic room an "unfinished" quality, the homeowners created a warm, friendly feeling by papering an end wall with a cheerful yellow print. The small painted panels between the rafters on the walls just below the roof were stenciled in a complementary floral design.

Soft-colored wallpaper can create a warm, cozy atmosphere in a country bedroom. The paper in the guest house bedroom above features a strawberry pattern. Tiny flowers mark the yellow paper in the California attic bedroom at right.

Country Florals

With their garden-inspired patterns and fresh outdoor look, floral-print wallpapers are synonymous with country style. The bedroom at left displays co-ordinated patterns: the paper used on the walls, striped with ribbons and nosegays, is a variation of the design on the ceiling paper. A cheery patterned paper accentuates the country feeling of the bathroom above.

A matching border links the complementary wallpapers used in the bedroom at left.

Painted white, a simple molding adds detail to the wallpapered bathroom above. New woven cotton rugs echo the green-and-pink color scheme.

OLD-STYLE WALLPAPERS

Handmade block-printed wall-papers, imported from England, first became available in this country around 1700. Many designs copied those of silk, damask, and tapestry wallcoverings; others were printed with motifs taken from the costly hand-painted scenic wallpapers then being made in China.

Even as imitations, fashionable imported wallpapers were a luxury that only the wealthiest colonists could afford. In fact, wallpaper still remained the province of the rich after 1760, when Americans began manufacturing their own. The first patterns produced here—floral repeats, like those on printed cottons—were freely borrowed from English and French papers. At the turn of the 18th century, interest in the excavations at Pompeii prompted designs that featured classical medallions, urns, and friezelike borders.

By the 1840s, the development of mechanized roller presses in America had revolutionized the printing process, and for the first time wallpapers were produced inexpensively. The Victorians—who considered plain white walls "the relics of barbarism"—took full advantage of the wider availability of wallpaper, often using as many as three patterns and two borders in a single room.

Today, many 18th- and 19th-century wallpaper and border patterns can still be purchased. Those shown here include both historically accurate reproductions and adaptations of early patterns. For more information on each paper, see page 170.

53

Moldings

Baseboard and cornice moldings should have the same proportions to balance each other.

A chair rail molding running about three feet above a baseboard adds dimension to a wall.

Used with wallpaper, a molding placed close to the ceiling can make a room seem loftier.

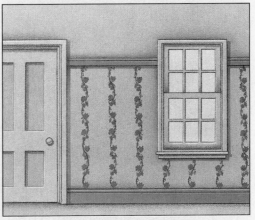

Used with wallpaper, a lowered molding can help break up the wall plane.

As interior details, moldings—decorative bands usually made of wood or plaster and used for cornices, baseboards, chair rails, and trim—give beauty to a room by adding dimension to otherwise flat surfaces and creating highlights and shadows.

A reflection of architectural tastes, molding styles too have changed with time. During the Federal period of the late 1700s and early 1800s, for example, designs borrowed from ancient Greece were in favor. By con-trast, during the Victorian era, fanci-fully ornate moldings with floral and scroll designs became popular.

The significance of moldings, how-ever, goes beyond the addition of decoration and period detail: they can also serve practical functions and solve design problems. Often, mold-ings are used to camouflage seams where different materials—wallpa-per and wood paneling, perhaps—are joined. They can also be used to change the appearance of a room's proportions. For example, painting a cornice (or ceiling-level) molding a darker shade than the background can make the ceiling appear lower. A white cornice molding next to a white ceiling can make a space feel loftier.

Lumber yards stock many stan-dard moldings, and a wide range of styles like those opposite—in plas-ter, wood, polystyrene, and pressed metal, which can be painted to match any decor—are also available by mail order through catalogs from spe-cialty companies.

Traditional Stencils

The stenciled motifs in the entry hall at right were applied over the entire wall to create the effect of wallpaper. While early stencilers cut stencils from heavy paper soaked in animal fat, artists today generally use acetate to make their templates.

Once the early settlers in America were able to think beyond bare necessities, they began introducing color and ornament into their homes. A treatment that became popular for walls was stenciling, which allowed people who were unable to afford the imported wallpapers that first became fashionable in the 1700s to imitate them with painted patterns. Such decorations, which were usually painted by itinerant artists in exchange for board and lodging, are often copied or adapted today.

The stenciling in the entrance hall opposite is based on patterns that were used by the 19th-century artist Moses Eaton, Jr. Here more than a dozen individual motifs have been combined to create the overall composition. In the bathroom above, a contemporary artist adapted other traditional motifs—diamonds and stars—for the chair rail and ceiling borders. She designed the tulip border over the sink herself.

The stenciled decoration in the bathroom above was limited to borders: the three different designs are linked by color and pick up the "colonial blue" of the woodwork.

Stenciled Borders

Used to define a wall pattern, or simply as a decorative frieze, a border was as important to early painted wall designs as the overall motifs; rarely was a room stenciled without one. The 19th-century artist who painted the parlor at left hardly lacked for border ideas: swags and tassels run along the top of the walls, flowers edge the baseboards and mantel, and diamonds follow the door frame. In the hall above, a stenciled swag design applied directly onto unpainted plaster intentionally contrasts with the floral checkerboard beneath: both were inspired by 18th-century motifs.

In an 1803 home, left, diamond border patterns were used to divide the wall into "panels."

The contemporary New England artist who created the wall pattern and border above painted the basic designs using stencils, then embellished the patterns freehand.

STENCILING A WALL BORDER

MATERIALS

· Flat latex or alkyd paint ·
(1 gallon covers approximately 350 square feet)
· Border stencils (precut, or your own design cut from clear .0075 acetate) ·
· Felt-tip pen for marking on acetate ·
· Japan paints (fast-drying varnish-based stenciling colors) in ½-pint cans ·
· Natural-bristle 1-inch stencil brushes, one for each paint color ·
· Roll of blank newsprint at least 1 foot wide ·
· Saucers for holding paints · Palette knife for mixing paints ·
· Masking tape · Paper towels · Mineral spirits for cleanup ·

◆

DIRECTIONS

1. Prepare walls with flat latex or alkyd paint (do not use high-gloss or semigloss).

2. Place japan paints in saucers, mixing with palette knife to achieve desired colors. Cover saucers with foil to keep paints from drying out. To avoid having to remix colors, prepare enough for entire border (¼ cup per color is sufficient for border of a 12- by 15-foot room). You should have a separate stencil for each color; colors are applied one at a time, beginning with largest motifs.

3. To determine placement of border on walls, first make a "proof" of stencil design. To make proof, affix stencil for first color to sheet of blank newsprint with masking tape. Dab stencil brush into paint, wiping off any excess on paper towel so that brush is almost dry. Apply paint to stencil in gentle circular motion. If bristles become dry and stiff, moisten paper towel with mineral spirits and apply to bristles.

4. After paint has dried, move stencil along, using registration marks on left or right side of stencil pattern to align for next design repeat. Continue until you have created a proof of first color that is 3 to 4 feet long. Repeat for all stencils in design until proof of design is complete.

5. Hold proof against wall to determine placement of border relative to ceiling. To mark final placement, make light pencil marks on wall and corresponding ink marks on stencil for first color.

6. For a continuous border like that shown here, start at dominant corner of room (the one your eyes see first when you enter). Tape stencil for first color to wall according to pencil marks, and apply paint as you did on proof (Illustration A). Move stencil along, using registration marks to align stencil for each repeat (Illustration B). Stencil first color along approximately two-thirds of wall, then use proof to measure how remaining design repeats will fall at next corner. If there is not enough room for entire design, you will need either to stretch it out or to squeeze it together unobtrusively by moving stencil ¼ inch to ½ inch per repeat during final third of the wall to fit design. Stencil first color around all walls.

7. Back at starting corner, tape stencil for second color to wall, using registration marks to align it over design made by first stencil. Apply paint using different brush (Illustration C). Stencil second color around all walls. Continue with all stencils that make up design (Illustration D). Clean stencils and brushes with mineral spirits.

A. First stencil is affixed with masking tape. Paint is applied in circular motion, building color.

B. Stencil can be moved along wall in either direction using registration marks.

C. Stencil for second color is registered over design for first color; new brush is used.

D. Subtle veining is added over previously stenciled leaves using third stencil.

Decorating doors was a typical practice in Swedish folk painting, a tradition that inspired the ornamentation in the Connecticut living room at right. According to the painted labels, the door marked "Gästkammare" leads to the guest bedroom, and the door marked "Köket" leads to the kitchen.

Folk-Art Painting

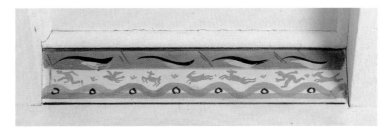

Painting freehand offers many decorating possibilities: it is an ideal way to tell a family story or evoke an ethnic look, and it can lend a feeling of cheerful exuberance to a room.

The paintings in the Connecticut house at left are by Erik Stocklassa, a 20th-century Swedish artist whose work recalls the traditional 18th- and 19th-century folk painting of his native country. In 1936 the original owner of the house commissioned Stocklassa to paint his living room in a manner typical of an old Swedish farmhouse, in which walls and doors were decorated with scenes inspired by family events, folktales, and biblical stories.

In a personal interpretation, Stocklassa included specific references to the Connecticut residence and the family who lived there. The large swag, which appears to be draped over the ceiling beams, includes the date of the artwork and the name of the street where the house is located. Amid the Swedish folk-art motifs of swirls, flowers, and vines, the owners themselves—dressed as 19th-century Swedish burghers—are depicted on the door panels.

In Swedish wall painting, narrow bands like those above were commonly used between rafters. The saying "Egen härd guld wärd," top, means "Your own hearth is worth gold." The humorous vignette, bottom, shows a country chase scene.

Country Murals

In the early 1800s, richly colored scenic wall-papers made in France were introduced to the American market, and it was not long before local artists began imitating them with painted landscape murals.

Like the papers, the murals were designed to connect related scenes in a continuous design around a room. Most were pastoral: according to a treatise by one well-known muralist, Rufus Porter, it was desirable that "a water scene . . . occupy some part of the walls. . . . Other parts, especially over a fire-place, will require more elevated scenes, high swells of land, with villages or prominent buildings."

Directly inspired by the work of Porter, the bedroom mural above and opposite was created by two contemporary artists for a 1789 New Hampshire house. The 19th-century painter's influence is clearly evident in the large, stylized trees and muted color scheme. And, like Porter's murals, this one is a composite of the real and the imaginary: the "high swells of land" over the mantel depict nearby hills; the "water scene" and homes are a fantasy.

Intriguing details on the fireplace wall above include blades of grass that appear to grow out of the chair rail and mantel.

Like their 19th-century counterparts, the modern-day "itinerant artists" who painted the bedroom mural opposite and above lived in the house while they worked.

RAGGING WALLS

Of all the paint treatments that can be used to create a country look for walls, ragging is one of the most subtle and elegant. In this "broken color" technique, thinned paint or glaze is brushed over a base coat, then pressed with a bunched-up rag or wad of paper toweling while still damp for a softly mottled, textured effect.

By changing the pressure and re-bunching the rags or towels, you can create gentle variations in pattern. The colors you choose will also affect the results. Using two colors rather than one will create a richer texture. On the wall above, for example, two shades of blue were ragged over a white base coat to create a cool, cloudy finish. For a more formal look, you might try neutrals: rag an off-white paint over a solid white ground. This creates a delicate finish that suggests the look of antique parchment. Two different colors can also be effective on a wall if you choose colors with values that are similar.

Experimenting is part of the fun, but whatever colors you select, be sure to use alkyd paint for the ragging colors. Alkyd paint has a better translucence than latex paint, which is too dense in body and dries too quickly to be used effectively in the process.

A. The ragging colors are applied with random brushstrokes so that the two shades overlap.

B. With wadded paper towels, the wet wall paint is ragged to create a mottled pattern.

C. The varied impressions made by the towels allow the base coat to show through the ragging colors.

MATERIALS

For a wall area measuring approximately 350 square feet, you will need one half gallon each of primer, base-coat paint, and mineral spirits. For ragging colors, you will need one quart for each color that you will be using.

- Alkyd or latex interior primer •
- Alkyd or latex low-luster enamel paint for base coat •
- 2 shades of alkyd low-luster enamel paint for ragging •
- Two 3-inch paintbrushes • 4 or 5 rolls of paper towels •
- 1 gallon odorless mineral spirits •
- 2 large containers for mixing paint •
- Plastic sheeting or painting tarpaulin •
- Masking tape •

DIRECTIONS

1. Spread plastic sheeting or painting tarpaulin on floor, and cover with masking tape any parts of window and door frames, moldings, fixtures, and baseboards that are adjacent to painting area. (Be sure to remove tape soon after paint has dried.)

2. Keeping work area well ventilated, prepare walls with one coat of primer according to manufacturer's directions, and let dry.

3. Cover walls with one coat of alkyd or latex base color according to manufacturer's directions, and let dry. Repeat with second coat.

4. In separate containers, dilute alkyd ragging colors with mineral spirits, mixing thoroughly until consistency is slightly thicker than heavy cream.

5. Working on 3-foot-wide sections at a time, and starting at top of wall, apply ragging colors from top to bottom of wall with brushes, alternating and overlapping colors. Use short strokes in random directions (Illustration A). Be sure to cover entire surface, and don't worry about paint looking messy.

6. While paint is still wet, wad about three sheets of paper towels together and begin pressing into paint so base color shows through (Illustration B). Work from top to bottom, ragging from edges of section toward middle to prevent paint buildup where sections will overlap. Rewad towels frequently; when they become clogged with paint, replace them with fresh ones. Finished section should have consistent ragged look (Illustration C).

7. Repeat steps 5 through 7 until all walls are covered.

TIPS

◆ Ragging walls is quicker and easier if two people work together: one person applies paint while the other person rags it.

◆ If you do work by yourself, be sure to limit yourself to 3-foot-wide sections so that paint won't dry before you can rag it.

◆ If doing an entire room, rag opposite walls first and let dry before doing other two walls to prevent smudging at corners.

◆ Make sure you have enough paper towels to complete your project. To keep them handy, tear towels off roll and pile them close to work area.

Pine Sheathing

The 18th-century corner cupboard above, which retains its original red paint, blends in well with pine wall sheathing from the same period.

From the time the colonists reached this country, pine sheathing was one of the most commonly used materials for finishing interior walls in New England homes. Most boards were sawed rather than hand-hewn (in fact, "sawyers" were listed among the first colonists) and then hand-planed to remove the saw marks. The pine sheathing in this Massachusetts home was salvaged from an 18th-century Connecticut house scheduled for demolition. The simple beveling used to finish the boards is known as featheredging.

Put up vertically, featheredged pine boards, right, create a chimney wall.

Wall Displays

Open shelving is not only a practical way to store belongings, but depending on the items displayed, it can also become the decorative focal point of a wall—or of an entire room.

Designed to accommodate an extensive collection of pewter, including English and American pieces, the simple built-in wall shelving that dominates one end of the dining room above is an integral part of the decor. Its rich green color allows each antique to stand out in an intriguing overall composition that adds interest and di-mension to the wall plane. The cornice that runs across the shelves and window serves as a plate rail for additional pieces.

In the 18th-century farmhouse living room at right, the unusual fireplace shelves, built directly against the slanting chimney, create a striking "overmantel," here filled with a collection of antique mochaware bowls, pitchers, and mugs. The dark red paint on the trim complements the pottery pieces, which date from the 1780s. Both the shelves and the flanking cupboards are original to the house.

Remodeled for display, the shelves in the Michigan dining room above hold pewter pieces, including flagons, chalices, and communion plates by Thomas Boardman, an early-19th-century Connecticut craftsman. The fireplace shelves at right, in a New Hampshire farmhouse, display antique mochaware.

Rustic Charm

For a rustic look, the squared-off hemlock timbers used for the walls of the log cabin bedroom at right were hand-finished using traditional tools.

A combination of hand-hewn beams and simple wall treatments gives a rustic feeling to these two inviting bedrooms. In the log cabin bedroom at left, the hemlock timbers used to construct the house were left exposed, then the walls, ceiling, and beams were painted white for a clean look.

The light paint brings out the interesting texture of the wood and helps make the space seem larger and brighter. The use of white also inspired the choice of light wood furnishings, which include a blond pine four-poster bed and a pine storage chest at its foot, both reproduction pieces.

In the bedroom above, located in a 19th-century Long Island farmhouse, the beams of the white wide-board ceiling were stained a pale blue gray to make them a more prominent feature in the room's decor. White walls create a fresh backdrop for additional touches of blue provided by the slate hearthstone and the antique pieced quilt.

White plaster walls, exposed ceiling beams, and a blue-and-white color scheme create a charming country feeling in the bedroom above, located in a restored 1830s Long Island house. To make the roughhewn beams stand out against the ceiling, they were stained blue gray.

Light from Above

A skylight can be a useful addition to any room of the home, supplementing ordinary windows, or bringing sunlight to a space where there were no windows at all.

In the 1740 farmhouse bedroom at left, the large skylight set into the sloping roof does much to brighten an attic room where two small, low windows originally offered the only light. To complement the rustic country look of the room, the skylight was finished with a hand-hewn frame, which was designed to blend in with the existing beams and was fitted with shutters held back with wrought-iron hooks.

In the bedroom above, simple contemporary skylights were installed in a row between the rafters. During peak hours of sun, the venetian blinds can be drawn shut to keep the antique pieced quilt from fading. Other antiques include the four-poster bed and an arrow-back rocker.

Skylights enhance the 18th-century farmhouse bedroom at left and its modern

counterpart in a Connecticut home above.

Country Floors

an important part of the country look

No decorating scheme is complete without attention to the floor: the basic materials, the painted decorations, or the rugs you choose can pull a decor together and have a significant effect on the tenor of a room. Today the possibilities for imaginative floors are seemingly endless, and while some treatments have a contemporary feeling, others find their inspiration in the past.

Early floor decorations, in fact, have a distinctive character and charm. Even as late as the mid-1800s, rugs were fairly uncommon in rural areas. Those that were used were made at home from the materials at hand: rush and straw, fabric remnants, rags. Another option for decorating floors was painting. Some painted designs imitated costly materials like marble, others were purely imaginative.

Both rugs and painted decorations are particularly well suited to today's country look. Your choices include antique rugs as well as a wide range of new braided, hooked, and rag rugs available in traditional designs. Or you might want to try a country paint treatment like spattering or stenciling. The ideas that follow should offer plenty of inspiration.

Hooked rugs form a patchwork of color against painted floorboards.

Traditional Wood Floors

The salvaged barnsiding used for the kitchen floor above was turned paint-side down, then polished on top to show off the natural beauty of the pine. Even a simple floor like this is an important element in a room's overall design.

In the 1600s, floorboards were worth so much that they were often laid down without nails so that they could be taken up easily when it was time to move. Today we are more likely to regard a floor as a decorative, rather than a monetary, investment. Even so, old wood is still valued—and often salvaged for reuse.

The pine floor in the 18th-century farmhouse kitchen above, for instance, was made from barnsiding. After purchasing the old boards, the homeowners planed them, then fixed them in place with handwrought rosehead nails.

The rustic one-room guest cottage at right was built almost entirely from materials recycled from other buildings. The wide pine floorboards were refinished with a translucent blue stain for a restful look; a coat of polyurethane provides an easy-maintenance finish.

The blue stain on the floor at right brings out the gold color of the painted 18th-century mantel.

A Checkered Past

During the colonial era, itinerant artists known as deception painters were commonly hired by homeowners to paint plain wood floors to look like they were made of fancier materials. One popular design was "counterfeit marble" tiles. "Any sort of marble is subject to your imitation," declared a 1688 treatise on decoration, "and, if neatly done... will in beauty and in gloss equal the real stone."

Today, as in the past, the designs for painted "tiles" are limited only by the imagination of the artists who produce them. The edges of the squares in the painted checkerboard opposite, for example, were scored into the paint to create the illusion of dimension. Above left, the floorboards showing through the paint lend an appealing folk quality to the green-and-white "marble" floor. The "inlaid marble" floor above right has variegated graining, with "grout" carefully painted along each tile edge.

The painted floor above left captures the feeling of marble without being an exact copy. The design above right was inspired by the floor pattern in a 19th-century painting.

A painted checkerboard floor can add drama as well as color to a room. The blue and beige "tiles" opposite complement the delicate wall mural and create a handsome setting for country furnishings.

SPATTER-PAINTING A FLOOR

Spatter-painting is an easy and relatively inexpensive way to give a scuffed wood or vinyl floor a charming new look. In this "free-form" painting technique, one or more colors of paint are showered from a brush to make spots that stand out against a solid background color. Depending on the colors you use and your individual spattering style, the result can be bright or muted, wild or subtle.

MATERIALS

For a floor measuring approximately 350 square feet, you will need one gallon each of primer, polyurethane, and mineral spirits and one or two gallons of base-color paint; for spattering, you will need one quart of paint for each color that you will be using.

· Primer to prepare floor for painting ·
· Flat alkyd paint for base color · Latex paints for spattering ·
· Polyurethane for protective finish ·
· Odorless mineral spirits ·
· 3-inch paintbrushes with stiff, squared-off bristles ·
(one for each color of paint used)
· Straightedged piece of wood, about 12 inches long ·
· Large sheets of drawing paper or newsprint ·
· Masking tape and/or plastic sheeting ·

◆

DIRECTIONS

1. Keeping work area ventilated, prepare floor with one coat of primer according to manufacturer's directions; let dry. Depending on porosity of floor, apply one or two coats of base paint according to manufacturer's directions; let dry.

2. Before spattering floor, practice your technique, trying out different sizes and densities of spatters on large sheets of paper. Thin the latex paint with water, if necessary, to make the paint the consistency of milk. Dip brush into paint until ends of bristles are lightly loaded with paint but not dripping. To spatter, hold piece of wood about one foot from surface of paper and tap metal part of brush handle sharply against edge of wood. To make larger spatters, hold wood closer to surface and tap in same manner.

3. Since paint tends to spatter over a wide area, protect baseboards and walls with masking tape and/or plastic sheeting. Spatter entire floor as you did paper, keeping density of spatters roughly the same. If you are using more than one color, the dominant color should be spattered on first and allowed to dry (Illustration A). Additional colors may then be spattered more sparsely on top (Illustration B). A natural variation in the size of the spots should be expected (Illustration C).

4. After paint has dried, protect spattering with polyurethane thinned with mineral spirits in equal parts. Apply two to three coats, letting each coat dry thoroughly between applications.

A. Metal part of brush handle is struck against piece of wood, spattering the paint. Size of spatters will vary.

B. A darker color spattered over a lighter one gives a feeling of depth. Use different brush for each color.

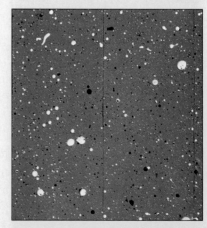

C. The variation in size and density of spatters creates an informal look. Use as many colors as you like.

Creative Stenciling

Probably no paint treatment offers as many possibilities for customized floor patterns as does stenciling. The basic technique is simple enough for anyone to learn, and can be elaborated upon as the artist becomes practiced.

The owners of a contemporary Minnesota saltbox wanted a simple floor pattern for their den, left, that would make the small room feel larger without competing with their collections of quilts, baskets, and toys. First-time stencilers, they copied a simple design from a friend's floor, cut the stencil themselves, and produced the gray-on-gray color scheme in latex paints.

The delicate stenciled design in the child's bedroom above, in a Connecticut farmhouse, was adapted from a medieval manuscript border by a professional artist using oil-base paints. For an ethereal quality, he stenciled the flowers in thin, transparent layers; the details and highlights were painted freehand. The pale yellow background suggests the look of old parchment.

Stenciled floors first became popular in America in the late 18th century and were relatively common until the mid-1800s. Today, stenciled designs like the traditional pattern at left and the delicate flowers above still offer a practical, colorful way to enliven a room.

Country Floor Cloths

The contemporary floor cloths above feature such traditional patterns as checks and diamonds. The rabbit design was inspired by motifs on antique Dedham pottery.

Known as floor cloths, painted and varnished canvas carpets like the colorful contemporary examples above and opposite were among the first floor coverings used in this country.

Initially brought over from England—probably as early as the 1600s—these decorative "rugs" originated as substitutes for more costly woven carpets and fine flooring materials like marble tiles and wood parquet. Extremely popular, they were favored in households both modest and grand until the late 1800s, when linoleum began to come into style. In particular, floor cloths were used in such heavily trafficked areas as halls and stairs; they were also laid over dining room carpets to protect them from spills.

An 1828 advertisement for floor cloths in the *New Hampshire Gazette* made the following claims: "These carpets possess a decided advantage over all others, as they are more durable, and in warm weather much more comfortable and easy to keep clean." Floor cloths were generally kept in place with tacks; when necessary, the rugs could be taken up and repainted.

According to the New Hampshire artist who made the colorful cloths shown here, they are equally practical today. "They're child- and pet-proof," she says, "and require minimal care."

*Used wall-to-wall,
canvas floor cloths, left,
create the effect of carpeting.
Smaller examples make
attractive area rugs or
wall hangings.*

Native
Ingenuity

Complete with traditional corner tassels, the painted "rug" in the dining room at right offers a stylized version of a Navajo design.

The striking floor treatments in these two country rooms were inspired by the rich tradition of Navajo Indian weaving, practiced by tribe members since the 17th century.

When the owner of the log cabin at left asked a professional artist to design a dining room floor that would complement her rustic collections, the painter responded with a Navajo "rug" stenciled directly onto the floorboards. The design recalls the bold patterns of Navajo weavings, interpreted in contemporary colors—a soft gray-blue background with white and tan accents. (White, brown, and indigo were the usual colors for Navajo rugs until the late 18th century, when the deep red now associated with them appeared.)

The textiles in the southwestern bedroom above are all Ganado-style weavings, named for the Arizona trading post where they were originally sold in the late 1800s. Such weavings are marked by their fine quality and gray, white, and red color scheme. Both of the rugs on the floor are Navajo-woven reproductions of early-20th-century originals; the smaller of the two took forty-eight days to complete. Weavings like the door curtains to the left of the bed are known as eye dazzlers, a term coined by early traders in reference to the textiles' characteristically intense colors and optically interesting designs, which often feature serrated zigzags.

The Navajo textiles in the bedroom above include two rugs—reproductions of early-20th-century pieces—and two "portieres," or door curtains, woven around 1910. By the 1880s, such traditional wool weavings were made mainly for sale to settlers and traders; earlier pieces are rare today.

Rag Rugs

With their warm, homespun look, rag rugs—traditionally made from fabric remnants or scraps of old clothing—are particularly at home in a country setting. While the rugs in this spacious bedroom were purchased as antiques, their variegated colors blend so well with the natural graining of the floor and wall paneling that the textiles ap-pear to have been specially made for the room.

The homeowner, who collects early American textiles, enjoys putting her pieces to everyday use. "Handmade rugs provide a lot of character that doesn't exist with modern carpeting," she says. Found in a Wisconsin log cabin, the runner opposite and the large rug in the sitting area above were woven as a set.

Made from scraps, early rag rugs were considered practical but expendable. Unusual care was taken with the pieced border on the carpet above.

In order to turn a corner, the long rag runner opposite was simply folded over itself. The hooked area rug by the bed was made by different hands, but its similar colors make it a compatible mate.

COLORFUL RAG RUGS

Like pieced quilts, woven rag rugs were the ingenious products of frugal, rural life. Made from salvaged pieces of old clothing and sheets, sewing scraps, and sometimes even purchased rags, their main attribute was their low cost; today, however, the rugs are prized for their beauty and durability.

Rag rugs were listed in American household inventories as early as the 1770s, but they reached the height of their popularity between the 1870s and 1930s. The Northeast and Canada were particularly well known for their colorful plaid, striped, and checked rugs; weavers throughout Pennsylvania and the Midwest produced heavier rugs, with random "hit-or-miss" colors.

Unlike quilts, which were usually made by women, rag rugs were often woven by men. Some were produced by family groups, or communally in "carpet bees." Others were made by itinerant weavers.

Wool and cotton were the most common fabrics for rugs, although linen and velvet were also used, and jute was popular in Canada; sometimes several types of fabric were combined in a single rug. The cloth was cut into long, narrow strips that were stitched end to end and used as a weft, or cross weave; the warp was made up of cotton, linen, or wool thread.

Most household looms were only large enough to make 36-inch-wide rugs, which were just the right width for carpeting a hallway or staircase. For a room-size carpet, several rugs were sewn together. When materials permitted, weavers produced two or three times the length of carpet needed, and the extra yardage was saved for use on special occasions or to replace a rug when it wore out.

Today, early examples of the durable and tightly woven rugs made in the Northeast are thought to be the finest. The rags used to weave their characteristically intricate plaids were often redyed for a more desirable color. The soft colors in such early rugs were created with natural dyes and can show considerable variation within a single weaving. In later rugs, commercial dyes produced consistent, but harsher, colors.

Before purchasing an old rag rug, examine it carefully. Normal signs of wear can be expected, but the individual fibers should still be intact and strong. Regular sweeping or shaking will keep your rugs clean. While old rag rugs should never be machine washed, they can be hosed down and dried on a flat surface. Rag rugs may also be dry-cleaned.

The rugs at right, dating from the 1880s to the 1930s, show the fine weaving and subtle, intricate patterns typical of northern New England and Canadian pieces.

Hooked
Rugs

Laid down in a random patchwork, the hooked rugs at right create an intriguing composition on bare wood floors.

When I wake up in the morning," says the owner of this house in rural Maine, "I get a charge out of seeing myself in the 19th century—or at least it's my own version of the 19th century."

His period furnishings include a collection of hooked rugs that is particularly well suited to the setting, since rug hooking is believed to have originated in coastal New England or Canada in the mid-1800s. And while the craft—which involves pulling fabric strips through a loosely woven backing—quickly caught on throughout

this country, it is still associated with the spare look of early New England interiors. Then, as now, the fancy patterns and thick nap of the wool rugs provided color and warmth in a room.

The area rugs in the bedroom, opposite, and the living room, above, date mainly from the early 1900s, but their elegant simplicity makes them thoroughly compatible with the 19th-century furniture. "When you get all the right furnishings together," the homeowner says, "a room starts to glow—it becomes more than the sum of its parts."

The early-20th-century hooked rugs above were purchased at an auction on Cape Cod. Although they were designed with matching patterns, the rugs are actually two different sizes.

Braided Rugs

The distinctive patterns in braided rugs result from the fabric colors and the braiding techniques: the multicolored 1930s piece above was made with five-strand braiding for a woven look.

Braided rugs, which are made from fabric strips that are entwined and then sewn together, originated in the early 19th century. The craft has been revived many times since, and the rugs—which lend themselves to various country looks—are still popular today.

The owner of the reproduction colonial house opposite let two old braided rugs inspire the traditional decor of her guest bedroom. "When I find an antique rug that I like," she says, "I'll decorate an entire room around it." Here the rugs are complemented by period fabrics: the plaid bedcover is made out of old cotton yard goods, and an 1800s indigo-and-white coverlet hangs on a green ladder by the window.

For the attic nursery above, in a Louisiana farmhouse, the homeowner chose a large braided rug from the 1930s. "It is perfect for a young child's room," she says, "because braided rugs are durable and they don't show stains."

Two oval braided rugs warm the bare floor of the bedroom opposite. These rugs were worked in three-strand combinations, the most typical braiding method for such textiles.

WOOD FLOOR TYPES

STRIP

◆ Strip flooring consists of narrow boards, generally less than 3 inches wide. The boards are usually ¾ inch thick and come in random lengths up to 8 feet; boards less than 18 inches long are called shorts. Common woods are white or red oak, maple, hickory, pecan, walnut, and teak. The boards are normally side- and end-matched (having tongue-and-groove joints on the ends as well as on the sides). They are graded according to quality: the higher the grade, the longer the boards and the fewer the color and grain variations. Strip is the most widely used type of wood flooring, and the most durable.

PLANK

◆ Plank flooring consists of boards 3 inches or more in width. The boards are usually ¾ inch thick and generally come in random widths up to about 7 inches and random lengths up to about 8 feet. The wider the board, the more consistency in grain and color. Common woods are white or red oak, fir, pine, and teak. Oak planks are normally side- and end-matched; planks of other woods are just side-matched. Plank floors are more susceptible than other flooring types to warping upward (cupping) or downward (bowing) and can gap along the edges of the boards as a result of excessive moisture.

PARQUET

◆ Parquet refers to any type of patterned wood flooring. It is made of custom-designed individual pieces, or prefabricated patterned tiles, laid down to create an overall geometric design. Typical patterns include basketweave, herringbone, and fingerblock (left). The tiles, usually ⁵/₁₆ inch thick, come in squares, rectangles, and hexagons, as well as in odd shapes, and are available in various stock sizes. Common woods are white or red oak, maple, walnut, and teak, which may be solid or veneered. Although it is strong, parquet is the least durable of wood flooring types.

EFFECT	INSTALLATION	CARE	COST
◆ Strip flooring is extremely versatile, suitable for casual and formal rooms alike. Ideally, the boards should run parallel to the long axis of a room. Using only shorts tends to make a room appear larger. Special effects can be achieved by creating borders with strips of different woods.	◆ Strip flooring should be blind-nailed (nailed invisibly in the side and end grooves) to a clean, moisture-proof, level subfloor; a plywood underlay is required when laying the boards on a concrete slab. Strip flooring must be laid over the floor joists at a 90-degree angle.	◆ Regular vacuuming or dry-mopping is required. A floor with a Swedish or a polyurethane finish should not be waxed; damp-mop with a solution of 2 cups of vinegar to 3 gallons of water. A floor with a wax finish should be machine-buffed. Soap or detergents should never be used.	◆ Strip flooring, sold by the square foot, is the best value in wood floors. Shorts are the least expensive type of strip, about the same price as 5/16-inch fingerblock parquet; top grade random-length oak strips are about twice as costly.
◆ Plank flooring is associated with a traditional or early American look, especially when wood dowels, plugs, or decorative nails are used to anchor the boards. Wide planks show off the graining of the wood.	◆ Plank floors should be nailed on the face or screwed down rather than blind-nailed, especially if the boards are wide or are not end-matched. Some planks can be glued. The subfloor should be sturdy and without flex; plywood is best. Plank floors must have adequate ventilation.	◆ Regular vacuuming or dry-mopping is required. A floor with a Swedish or a polyurethane finish should not be waxed; damp-mop with a solution of 2 cups of vinegar to 3 gallons of water. A floor with a wax finish should be machine-buffed. Soap or detergents should never be used.	◆ Plank, sold by the square foot, is the most expensive type of wood flooring. The flooring varies greatly in price, depending on the width of the boards, and whether soft- or hardwood is used; 3- to 7-inch-wide random-length oak planks can cost up to twice as much as strip flooring.
◆ Parquet flooring can have a formal or casual look, depending on the pattern, the wood type, and the use of decorative borders. With its multidirectional patterns, parquet is less likely to draw attention to a floor with irregular dimensions than is strip or plank flooring.	◆ Some parquet tiles come with self-stick backing; others must be glued down. Parquet should be laid on a clean, level subfloor with a porous surface and no flex; most can be laid directly on concrete. Prefabricated panels are relatively easy to apply; custom pieces require a professional.	◆ Regular vacuuming or dry-mopping is required. A floor with a Swedish or a polyurethane finish should not be waxed; damp-mop with a solution of 2 cups of vinegar to 3 gallons of water. A floor with a wax finish should be machine-buffed. Soap or detergents should never be used.	◆ Parquet tiles, which are usually sold by the square foot, are the least expensive type of wood flooring. Prices increase with the intricacy of patterns and special effects such as borders. Custom designs are extremely expensive, from five to ten times as costly as the do-it-yourself tiles.

Oriental Rugs

Oriental carpets were among the most prized possessions of the colonists. Persian rugs and "Turkey carpitts" were so precious, in fact, that until the 1760s they were never used on the floor, but were instead proudly displayed on tables and chests. Today, no oriental carpets are known to have survived from the colonial period, but examples from the 1800s and early 1900s abound.

An early-20th-century Heriz carpet provides the decorative focal point in the sparely fur-

nished library above. Named for a village in the region of northwest Iran where they have been woven since at least the early 19th century, Heriz carpets are characterized by medallions and stylized flowers and leaves.

The collection of oriental rugs in the 1705 New England house opposite includes the late-19th-century Heriz in the foreground, topped by a smaller rug fragment from a neighboring region of Iran. The rug in the adjacent entry hall is a Kerman, woven in southeast Iran.

A Heriz carpet from the early 1900s provides bright color in the paneled library above. Its deep reds and blues set off the rich woods of an antique Queen Anne table and a pair of Windsor chairs.

When oriental carpets wear out, fragments are often saved. The small rug by the door, opposite, is a section of a Persian rug; an even smaller rug fragment is displayed on the table.

Solid Footing

The natural look of a brick or stone floor can help bring an outdoor feeling indoors. In the dining room at left—built as an addition to a remodeled 18th-century barn—salvaged bricks were chosen to complement the rustic character of the old building. The homeowners particularly enjoy the room during the summer months: the bricks stay cool underfoot and help to enhance the greenhouse-like atmosphere in the sunny, plant-filled space.

Bluestone was used to pave the entry hall of the Long Island vacation house above. The random shapes of the stone create a terracelike effect and provide a fitting transition from yard to house. While the hard-wearing floor is practical for a high-traffic area, its rugged look is also compatible with the floral chintz curtains, botanical prints, and Victorian furnishings.

Laid in pairs, bricks create a simple geometric pattern for the dining room floor at left. Bluestone, used to pave the entry hall above, is not only durable but sophisticated.

Country Fabrics

homespuns, ginghams, calicoes, linens, laces, and more

One of the greatest pleasures in country decorating is choosing fabrics for such furnishings as curtains, upholstery, slipcovers, bed dressings, and table coverings. Among the wide variety of new country fabrics available today are nubby cottons and linens that recall the look and texture of the simple homespuns that were made well into the 1800s from yarns spun and woven by hand. Other favorites include calicoes and chintzes, which were particularly popular in the 19th century and are still admired for their appealing designs.

While many of these new fabrics are beautiful and relatively inexpensive, there is also something special about incorporating antique pieces into a country decor. An old shawl or a fragment of vintage lace draped over a table or a chair back can add a touch of nostalgia to a room. And although early quilts and coverlets may command high prices, even one good piece, thoughtfully displayed, can make a room come alive.

Quilts, lace, and chintz bring a country feeling to a city bedroom.

Homespun Decor

The antique homespun remnants above reveal the range of plaids and checks that could be turned out by early weavers. The yarns, usually made from cotton, flax, or wool and prepared at home, were colored with indigo and other natural dyes.

The owner of this 1830s log home has decorated his guest bedroom with homespuns, the basic homemade fabrics woven from cotton, flax, and wool that were standard in rural households from the earliest days of the colonies until well into the 1800s.

The simple patterns of these utilitarian fabrics are particularly well suited to the cabin's rustic decor. Some of the antique pieces, like the remnants in the cupboard above, are reserved for display. Others, right, are used as they would have been in earlier days: for curtains, bed tickings, even schoolbook covers.

Two 19th-century dresses and a calico bonnet complement the homespuns in the bedroom, right.

CALICO

The daintily patterned cottons that we call calico are probably most often associated with patchwork quilts and pioneers' bonnets. But this popular "American" fabric actually originated in India.

Calico takes its name from the port of Calicut, on India's southwest coast. The term first referred to any cotton, printed or plain, shipped from there after trade was established with the East in 1498. At some point—no one knows just when—"calico" came to mean any hand-painted or dyed cotton, usually with a floral pattern, made in India.

The first of these lightweight, cool, and often colorful fabrics arrived in Europe in the early 1600s. Westerners were immediately taken with the new, unfamiliar cotton, and European fabric makers soon learned to imitate the Indian patterns with block printing. Americans adopted the block printing technique as well: colonial calico printers advertised their wares as early as 1712.

Calico as we now know it—characterized by small, all-over repeated patterns—emerged in the early 1800s with the improvement of mechanized weaving machines and the development of roller printing processes. The technology enabled New England mills to turn out millions of bolts of the fabric, which once sold for five cents a yard.

Pretty, inexpensive, and easy to launder, calico became popular in the 19th century for both clothing and household goods. The vintage items at left include yardage, a dress, quilt squares, and a drawstring seed bag.

Silks
and Laces

The sheer silk shawl draped
from the top of the window
above adds a look of softness
without blocking the view
of the yard beyond.

Delicate fabrics purchased at flea markets and auctions lend a light air to this cottage sunroom. Here the homeowners simply experimented with their unmatched finds until each had a "home." Draped over the sofa, one shawl, for example, becomes a throw; another, layered under a lace cloth, serves as an unusual skirt for the round occasional table.

Fine fabrics were used equally effectively for window treatments. An embroidered silk shawl, above, and handmade lace runners caught near their ends, right, make graceful curtains: their delicate patterns are accentuated by changes in light and shadow.

Lace runners and fringed shawls complement chintz
fabric and add romance to the sunroom, right.

110

Traditional Curtains

Curtains, one of the most important fabric treatments in a room, can contribute considerably to the mood that a decor conveys. By recalling traditional early American styles, these two window treatments bring a period flavor to two different settings.

For the formal swag curtains, left, the fabric was gathered on a rod, with elegant "tails" hanging at the sides. The more casual festoon curtain, above, is made from a simple panel; a cord passed through a series of rings sewn on the back is pulled to gather the fabric.

The formal look of swag curtains, left, was especially fashionable in the early 19th century.

Used extensively in 18th-century America, festoon curtains like the one above were favored because they could be made from relatively little fabric. Such curtains were often nailed right to the window frame.

Choosing Curtains

Hardware and trimmings can be as important to curtain design as the fabric. The swag above left is caught with brass hearts; tiebacks, above right, suit the simple look of tab curtains.

The style of curtain you choose depends on a number of things, among them your fabric preferences, the shape, size, and location of the window, privacy needs, and the amount of natural light that you want to let into a room. The curtain treatments on these pages are just a few of the many styles that can work well with a country decor.

The window above left, in a farmhouse sitting room, frames a rural view and admits plenty of afternoon sunlight. Here, a traditional swag—in which the fabric is caught at the corners of the window and neatly draped—was a good choice: the curtain softens the window, yet leaves most of it uncovered, and it lets the handsome woodwork stand out as an important decorative element.

Tab curtains, like those above right, have been popular since the late 1700s because they are easy to sew and do not require much fabric.

The floral-stripe pattern chosen for these curtains was carefully color-coordinated with the soft gold of the 19th-century-style molding, the window frame, and the chair rail.

The tieback curtains above left copy a 19th-century style and were selected because they are compatible with the traditional decor of the 1823 house. Gathered on a rod, the loosely woven cotton fabric billows over self ties and is drawn back in deep folds to reveal the original twelve-over-twelve double-hung windows.

A swag curtain like the one above right takes on an informal look when a simple ticking-stripe pattern is used and the fabric is casually draped. This variation on the traditional swag was achieved by pulling a length of polished cotton loosely through iron rings at the window corners. The blue stripe in the fabric picks up the color of the stenciled borders and of the painted woodwork.

Stenciled wall borders can enhance the country look of a curtain treatment. The swaglike stencil motifs above left echo the drape of the fabric; vines and leaves complement the striped cotton "ticking" above right.

Kitchen Fabrics

Before the advent of draw curtains in the 1820s, tiebacks were typically used for pulling back a curtain to admit more light. The ties looped over the curtain rod above are an imaginative variation on the more customary side tie.

With their color and softness, simple fabric treatments take the utilitarian edge off these two country kitchens. To set a homey feeling in the 19th-century-style Ohio keeping room above, the owner chose tab curtains in a plaid cotton that resembles homespun; they are hung from a traditional wooden dowel rod.

In the antiques-filled Louisiana kitchen at right, softly gathered fabric panels—in a French provincial print—replace the original screens in the old cypress wall cabinets. A skirt made from the same fabric was used to camouflage an under-counter storage area.

Casual cotton in a cheerful blue print enhances the airy look of the kitchen at right.

TAB CURTAINS

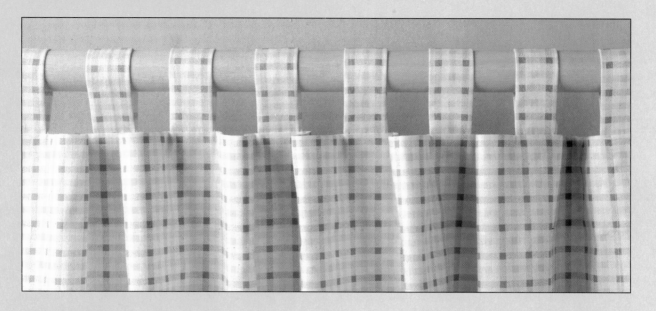

MATERIALS

(See directions for amounts)

- Medium-weight fabric such as linen or chintz
- Dressmaker pins

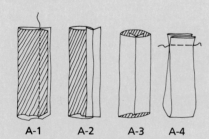

| A-1 | A-2 | A-3 | A-4 |

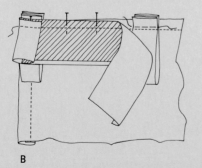

B

DIRECTIONS

1. Install dowel-type curtain rod.

2. For one pair of curtains, cut two fabric panels. To calculate length of each panel, measure desired curtain length from top of rod. To calculate width, measure rod and multiply by ¾. For facings, cut two 3-inch-wide strips of fabric to same measurement as panel width. For each tab, cut a fabric piece 3½ inches x 7 inches. You will need one tab for approximately every 5 inches of curtain rod.

3. To make tabs for each panel, fold each piece in half lengthwise with right sides together. Machine-stitch ½-inch seam along long edge (Illustration A-1). Iron seam open (A-2). Turn tab right side out, center seam, and iron (A-3). Bring open ends together with raw edges even and seam inside, and stitch ⅜-inch seam along raw edges (A-4).

4. Begin making curtains by hemming bottom and side edges of each panel. At each side edge, turn under 1¼ inches to wrong side and iron; turn under ¼ inch at raw edge, pin, and stitch. Remove pins. At bottom, turn under 2½ inches to wrong side and iron; turn under ¼ inch at raw edge, pin, and stitch. Remove pins.

5. Pin tabs to top of each panel. With raw edges of tabs aligned with raw edges of panel (tabs hanging down), place one tab at each side hem; space others evenly in between. Machine-baste tabs in place, ⅜ inch from edge; remove pins.

6. Turn under ¼ inch of one long edge of facing strip to wrong side and iron. Turn ends of strip under so that strip measures same as width of panel, and iron. With right sides together, pin raw edge of facing to top of curtain, over tabs. Stitch ½-inch seam along top (Illustration B). Remove pins, flip the facing to wrong side of curtain so that tabs turn upward, and pin turned-under edge of facing to wrong side of curtain; stitch. Remove pins and iron heading. Sew open ends of facing together by hand.

7. Slide tabs over curtain rod.

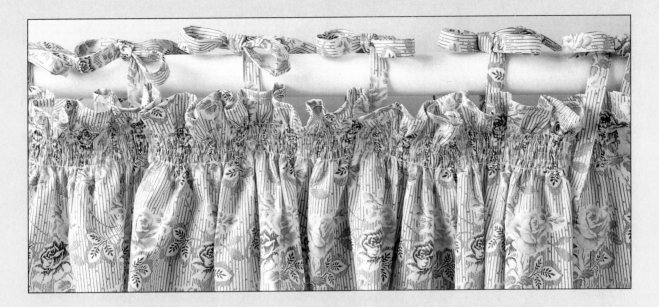

DIRECTIONS

1. Install dowel-type curtain rod.

2. For one pair of curtains, cut two fabric panels. To calculate length of each panel, measure desired curtain length from top of rod and add 3½ inches. To calculate width, measure rod and multiply by 1¼. For each tie, cut a fabric strip 2 inches x 30 inches. You will need one tie for approximately every 4 inches of curtain rod.

3. To make ties for each panel, turn under ½ inch on each end to wrong side and iron (Illustration A-1). Fold tie in half lengthwise with wrong sides together and iron (A-2). Open tie and fold each raw edge to center crease and iron (A-3). Refold lengthwise (A-4) and machine-stitch ⅛ inch in along the three open edges.

4. Begin making curtains by hemming edges of each panel. At top, turn under ¼ inch twice, pin, and stitch. Remove pins. At each side edge, turn under 1¼ inches to wrong side and iron; turn under ¼ inch at raw edge, pin, and stitch. Remove pins. At bottom, turn under 3 inches to wrong side and iron; turn under ¼ inch at raw edge, pin, and stitch. Remove pins.

5. To shirr top of each panel, draw light pencil line on right side of fabric 1¼ inches below top edge, stopping at side hems; machine-baste along line. Stitch five parallel rows of basting ¼ inch apart below first. To mark tie placements, fasten a safety pin on right side of fabric next to lines of basting on hem allowance, ½ inch from each side edge (Illustration B). Between these two pins, space more safety pins at even intervals, about 8 inches apart.

6. Pull wrong-side threads of top two lines of basting, and adjust gathers so that panel measures half the rod length and safety pins are equally spaced. Repeat for the two middle and two bottom basting rows.

7. On wrong side, pin a tie across rows of basting at each safety pin so that top end of tie is 14 inches from bottom row (Illustration C). Remove safety pins. Stitch along top and bottom rows of basting to secure ties and gathers. Remove pins.

8. Tie ties in bows around curtain rod.

MATERIALS

(See directions for amounts)

- Lightweight or sheer fabric, such as gingham or dimity
- Hard lead pencil for drawing on fabric
- Dressmaker pins
- Small safety pins

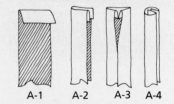

A-1 A-2 A-3 A-4

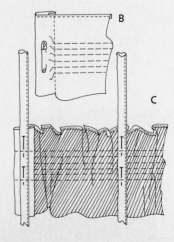

B

C

LACED CURTAINS

MATERIALS

(See directions for amounts)

- Medium-weight fabric such as linen or chintz
- ¼-inch eyelets and eyelet maker
- ¼-inch cord, such as cable cord or lacing, at least twice the length of the rod
- 2-inch-wide iron-on interfacing
- Dressmaker pins

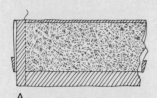

A

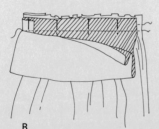

B

DIRECTIONS

1. Install dowel-type curtain rod.

2. For one pair of curtains, cut two fabric panels. To calculate length of each panel, measure desired curtain length from top of rod and add 1½ inches. To calculate width, measure rod and add 2 inches. For bands, cut two fabric strips, each 5 inches wide and 2 inches longer than half the rod measurement. Cut two strips of 2-inch-wide interfacing, each 1 inch shorter than band.

3. To make band for each panel, fold one fabric strip in half lengthwise with right sides together; iron. Pin strip of interfacing to wrong side of fabric strip with one long edge at fold and other three edges ½ inch from raw edges of strip; iron to fuse. Remove pins. Turn fabric strip over and turn up ½ inch on long raw edge; iron. Machine-stitch ½-inch seam at each short end (Illustration A). Turn band right side out and iron.

4. Begin making curtains by hemming bottom and side edges of each panel; at each side edge turn under 1 inch to wrong side and iron; turn under ¼ inch at raw edge, pin, and stitch. Remove pins. At bottom, turn under 3 inches to wrong side and iron; turn under ¼ inch at raw edge, pin, and stitch. Remove pins.

5. To assemble each curtain, machine-baste ½ inch from raw edge of top, stopping at side hems. Repeat, ¼ inch from raw edge. With right sides together and raw edges even, pin interfaced side of band to top edge of curtain, starting at ends, then matching centers of panel and band. Pull wrong-side threads of basting, and adjust gathers to distribute fullness evenly. Pin band to curtain, and stitch ½-inch seam (Illustration B). Remove pins; press band upward. Fold band over curtain top, and hand-hem folded edge to wrong side of curtain along seam line.

6. To mark locations for eyelets, center pin on band ¾ inch from each end; between these two pins, space more pins at even intervals, about 4 inches apart. Following directions that accompany your eyelet maker, apply ¼-inch eyelet at each mark.

7. Knot one end of cord. Lace cord through eyelets and slide loops over rod. Knot other end of cord; cut off excess.

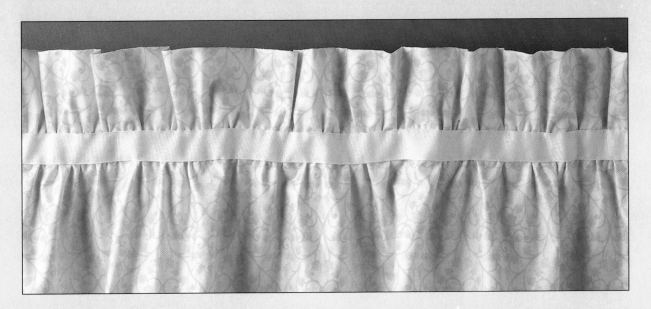

DIRECTIONS

1. Install ½-inch projection-type curtain rod.

2. For one pair of curtains, cut two fabric panels. To calculate length of each panel, measure desired curtain length from top of rod and add 10 inches. To calculate width, measure rod and multiply by ¾.

3. Begin making curtains by hemming edges of each panel. At each side edge, turn under 1 inch to wrong side and iron; turn under raw edge ¼ inch, pin, and stitch. Remove pins. At bottom, turn under 3 inches and iron; turn under raw edge ¼ inch, pin, and stitch. Remove pins. At top edge, turn under 3¾ inches to wrong side and iron; turn under ¼ inch at raw edge, pin, and hem by hand. Remove pins. On wrong side, place a pin into hem at center of curtain and at edges, and halfway between center and each edge to divide into quarters.

4. Machine-baste ⅜ inch above hem edge between pin at side edge and next pin; machine-baste again ¼ inch above first line of stitching. Repeat for each quarter. Pull wrong-side threads of machine basting and adjust gathers in each quarter until panel measures half the rod length. Stitch between rows of basting to hold gathers in place.

5. Measure ribbon to width of each gathered panel, adding 2 inches, and cut. Baste top edge of ribbon to panel 2½ inches below curtain top, turning raw ends of ribbon under 1 inch (see illustration). Stitch in place along top edge of ribbon, then along bottom.

6. Pin curtain hooks or hand-sew rings to wrong side of curtain behind ribbon, placing one at each edge, then spacing others at even intervals, approximately 3 to 4 inches apart. Slide rings or hooks over rod.

MATERIALS

(See directions for amounts)

- Light- or medium-weight fabric such as calico or gingham
- Satin or grosgrain ribbon, about 1 inch wide
- 1-inch curtain hooks or 1-inch-diameter sew-on rings
- Dressmaker pins

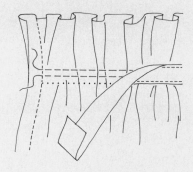

Furniture Fabrics

The success of any piece of upholstered or slipcovered furniture depends on how well the fabric you select relates to the character of the piece itself and to your overall decor. Practicality can also be an important consideration when picking a fabric: tightly woven, medium-weight fabrics such as cotton, nylon, and acrylic, for instance, are particularly good choices because they are durable. And when chosen in dark colors with a slight texture, they are less apt to show signs of wear.

Color and pattern should also be considered in your selection of fabric. The boldly printed cotton used to upholster the furniture in the comfortable family room at left was picked with both practicality and design in mind. The dark, sturdy fabric holds up well in the much-used room and introduces dramatic splashes of color amid the setting of pastels and neutrals. Used on all the major seating pieces, the fabric also lends a uniform feeling to the decor. Pillows in a quiet plaid and a woven checkerboard-pattern throw are effective accents.

In the bedroom sitting area above, the choice of bold fabrics and patterns produces a different atmosphere: the complementary flowered chintzes on the chair slipcover and pillow, the crisp check for the curtains, and the delicate lace for the tablecloth all work together here to achieve a casual, eclectic effect.

In the family room at left, the dark tones of the upholstery are balanced by the neutrals in the rush rug and muslin curtains. Checked and flowered fabrics mix well in the bedroom above.

Elegant Fabrics

Fabrics are the focal point of the decor throughout this New England house, where floral chintzes, delicate window treatments, and soft, woven floor coverings contribute to a quiet, elegant feeling.

In the master bedroom above, a pretty chintz in a cabbage rose pattern was used for a pillow and for cushions on the window seat and Empire-style pine bench. Billowy balloon shades dress the windows, and a lilac-striped rag rug picks up the subtle color scheme. An antique rag rug, soft from washing, serves as a bedcover.

In the sitting room, right, the crisp green-and-white madras upholstery on the settee coordinates with the polished cotton that covers the pair of armchairs. Draped asymmetrically, white voile with a satin stripe makes graceful curtains for the door and window.

Above, pastel fabrics are set off by pale pink bedroom walls. In the sitting room at right, florals and stripes stand out against walls of deeper pink painted with trompe l'oeil pilasters and wood graining.

A Fabric Glossary

◆*burlap* A coarse, sturdy plain-weave fabric made from a fibrous plant such as jute, flax, or hemp. Burlap is typically used to make upholstery backings and to cover furniture springs.

burlap

◆*calico* A tightly woven cotton plain-weave fabric. In the 18th century, calicoes were often solid-colored or white; today the name generally refers to cotton fabrics with a small, repeated pattern.

◆*canvas* A strong, heavy fabric tightly woven from cotton, hemp, or flax. Available bleached, dyed, or in the natural color of the fiber used to make it, canvas has a crisp look that is well suited to upholstery and slipcovers.

◆*chintz* A tightly woven cotton plain-weave fabric printed with bright patterns that are usually composed of no fewer than five colors. The name "chintz" comes from the word *chitta,* meaning "spotted cloth," which re-ferred to the painted and printed fabrics made in 17th-century India. Chintz is generally glazed for a lustrous finish.

chintz

◆*corduroy* A durable woven fabric made of cotton or synthetics and characterized by lengthwise ribs, or wales, that may vary in width. The name comes from the French phrase *corde du roi,* or "the king's cord," a reference to the fabric made for the king's servants during the Middle Ages.

◆*cotton* A fabric, available in many weights and weaves, made from thread that has been spun from the fiber of the cotton plant. Muslin, calico, and chintz are all cottons.

◆*crewelwork* A richly textured embroidery, usually done with wool yarn on an unbleached cotton or linen fabric. Crewelwork is used to decorate pillows, curtains, and upholstery.

crewelwork

◆*damask* A reversible fabric, usually made of linen, silk, or wool, characterized by a flat jacquard-weave pattern. Tablecloths and napkins are often made of damask.

◆*denim* A durable, tight twill-weave fabric, usually made of cotton, in which the warp is a color—traditionally blue—and the weft is white.

◆*dimity* A thin, crisp fabric woven from cotton, usually with checks or raised stripes or ribs. Dimity is often used for curtains, upholstery, and slipcovers.

◆*flame stitch* A distinctive textile pattern, also known as Irish stitch, characterized by irregular, zigzag lines and subtle color gradations that suggest the look of flames.

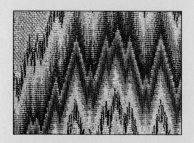

flame stitch

◆*flannel* A soft, twill-weave fabric, usually made of cotton, wool, or a synthetic blend, with a nap on one or both sides.

◆*foulard* A lightweight fabric, made of silk or rayon, characterized by a soft feel; usually printed with small figures on a solid background.

◆*gingham* A light- to medium-weight, plain-weave cotton in which the characteristic checked, striped, or plaid patterning is woven into the fabric rather than printed onto it.

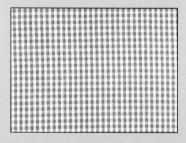

gingham

◆*glaze* The sheen or glossy finish produced by treating a fabric with starch, glue, paraffin, or synthetic resin during manufacture. Polished cotton is a glazed fabric.

◆*homespun* A loosely woven plain-weave fabric made of unevenly spun yarns of cotton, wool, or flax that give it a nubby texture. Homespun is often woven in a simple pattern such as a stripe or plaid. In America, the term "homespun" originally referred to the fabrics that were commonly produced on hand looms at home until the mid-1800s. While homespun may also be machine-made today, the cloth still retains the rough, simple look that characterizes its namesake.

◆*jacquard weave* A complex, decorative weave characterized by raised reverse-and-repeat patterns. Originally used to make bed coverlets, the jacquard weaving technique was developed in France and introduced in this country by the 1820s. Today, the jacquard weave is often used to produce the richly patterned cottons and linens favored for napkins and tablecloths.

jacquard weave

◆*lace* A delicate, openwork fabric made by looping, twisting, or knotting threads into decorative patterns. Lace is often used for pillows, tablecloths, and curtains.

◆*linen* A strong, lustrous woven fabric made from the fibers of the flax plant. Available in many weights and weaves, linen is often used for curtains, napkins, and tablecloths.

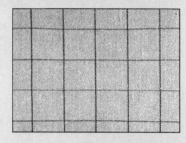

linen

◆*moiré* A lustrous fabric finish characterized by an irregular wavy, or waterlike, pattern. Traditionally found on ribbed silk, the moiré finish is also used on synthetic fabrics.

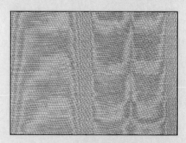

moiré

◆*muslin* A plain-weave cotton fabric that is usually bleached white or left in its natural off-white color, but may also be printed or dyed.

◆*nap* A soft, fuzzy surface that is produced by lifting the fibers from the fabric surface after the weaving is complete. Such twill weaves as flannel are often made with a nap.

◆*pile* A soft fabric surface, produced during the weaving process, in which a mass of raised loops or tufts is formed by extra warp or weft yarns.

◆*plain weave* The most basic type of weave, in which the warp and weft threads are about the same weight and are alternately passed under and over each other. Muslin, gingham, burlap, calico, homespun, and chintz are all plain-weave fabrics.

◆*seersucker* A light fabric of linen or cotton, usually with alternating plain and puckered stripes.

◆*silk* A strong, lustrous fabric made from the fiber of the silkworm cocoon. Silk is made in a variety of weaves, including plain and jacquard; the finishes may be "raw," or nubby in texture, as well as ribbed, moiré, or smooth and glossy.

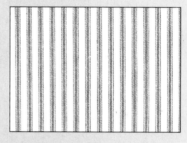

ticking

◆*ticking* A heavy cotton or linen twill-weave fabric, often characterized by a lengthwise stripe. Ticking is a traditional covering for mattresses and pillows.

◆*twill weave* A basic textile weave that produces an overall surface pattern of fine parallel lines or ribs, usually running on the diagonal.

◆*velvet* A soft, luxurious fabric made of wool, silk, cotton, or a synthetic, and characterized by a smooth pile on one side.

◆*warp* The parallel, lengthwise yarns or threads of a woven fabric.

◆*weft* The yarns or threads that run perpendicular to the warp. Also known as filling yarns.

◆*wool* A fabric made from the dense, soft, curly hair of the domesticated sheep; a good insulator.

Decorated Beds

Bed furniture—as the canopies, curtains, blankets, spreads, and skirts used to cover beds for privacy and warmth during colonial times were called—was considered among the most valuable of household belongings. Today these articles are often the inspiration for imaginative fabric treatments.

Flowered chintz and deep ruffles, for example, distinguish the romantic dressings on the pine tester bed at left. The skirt, canopy, curtains, and pillow shams, detailed with red welting, and the matching fabric used for the shades and sofa, give the room a sumptuous look. The wool coverlet, a new piece from Wales, adds a pleasing contrast of texture.

In the bedroom above, a summery feeling was achieved by draping the pine pencil-post bed with two delicate cutwork blanket covers—one used for the bedspread, the other laid loosely over the top of the bed frame as a canopy. Lacy pillow shams add subtle pattern to the all-white color scheme.

The chintz canopy in the bedroom at left helps divert attention from a large beam that the homeowners

found unsightly. The lacy tester above creates a textured "ceiling."

Quilts and Coverlets

Traditional quilts and coverlets, which often incorporate strong patterns and bright colors, can be distinctive additions to the decor of a country-style bedroom.

The overshot coverlet on the pencil-post bed opposite was selected because its brilliant colors coordinate with the stenciled wall border. Another coverlet, an 1851 jacquard weave folded at the foot of the bed, and pillows covered in old quilt and coverlet remnants provide contrast.

The homeowner who furnished the bedroom above for her daughter believes in using—rather than just displaying—her collection of quilts: here, different pieces contribute visual interest to the simple setting. The star quilt on the antique child's bed in the corner is a family heirloom. The red-and-green Ohio quilt on the larger bed displays a Triple Irish Chain pattern.

Pieced and appliqué quilts give a warm, comfortable feeling to a child's bedroom, above, and still hold up well under use.

The woven bedspread opposite is a 19th-century overshot coverlet, so called because some of the weft, or filler, yarns skip—or "overshoot"—the warp yarns to create a distinctive pattern.

131

INDIAN PATTERN BLANKETS

Among the most popular of American textiles collected today are Indian pattern blankets like the early-20th-century examples at left. Even more interesting than their distinctive patterns—inspired primarily by Navajo blanket designs—is the history behind such pieces.

By the turn of the century, several manufacturers of woolen textiles, including the Pendleton Woolen Mills and the Oregon City Mills in the Northwest, had started making "Indian pattern" blankets and selling them to the Indians.

Patterned blankets, which were worn as ceremonial robes, played a critical role in the culture of many tribes, and were considered an important measure of wealth. A single handwoven blanket, however, could take up to a year to make, and it became clear to the tribespeople that it was more sensible to barter the handwoven pieces at trading posts and buy the mill-produced ones for their own use. The manufactured blankets soon became as important to the Indians as the handwoven pieces had been. Some companies did make cotton blankets for a non-Indian market, but even today over 80 percent of the new Indian pattern blankets that are mill-produced are sold to Indians.

There is currently a strong market for vintage Indian pattern blankets like the 1920s examples at left, made of wool and cotton.

Finishing Touches

*the personal accents that
complete the look of a room*

Whether they be baskets of fresh flowers, a stack of colorful bandboxes, or a collection of samplers, the right accessories can bring character to a decor and strike a country mood in almost any setting. When adding these finishing touches to your home you will find that you are limited only by your imagination.

Indeed, almost any items that are not major furnishings—decorative objects, artworks, collectibles, lighting fixtures—can be considered accessories. The options for arranging such pieces are equally varied. For emphasis, you may want to use a piece alone, but accessories are also effective when grouped—on walls, shelves, floors, and stairways, or atop a desk or table. You can also arrange individual items by theme, color, or style, or create an eclectic mix. Changed according to season, perhaps, or simply upon whim, your arrangements are entirely a matter of personal taste. And, as you will see on the following pages, country accessories do not have to be elaborate. Even simple glass bottles, wooden butter molds, or a few pretty bowls can make effective accents.

A grouping of kitchen collectibles becomes an appealing still life.

Attractive Displays

Four varied gilded and painted frames set off the 19th-century portraits displayed over the staircase, above, and become an important part of the overall look of the arrangement.

While a work of art often deserves to be displayed individually, grouping pieces—by style, subject matter, or even the kind of frame—can also show them off to advantage and create an impact in a room.

The sizes of the 19th-century portraits hung over the staircase above are all different, as are the frames, yet the arrangement is successful because the works are related by their "primitive" feeling. To accommodate the awkwardly shaped wall space, the homeowners arranged the paintings asymmetrically.

Downstairs, they planned their family room, opposite, to include a "gallery" for an extensive collection of antique samplers. By placing a number of pieces on one wall, they created an impressive overall composition in which each painstakingly embroidered sampler still stands on its own. The narrow space between the door and a cupboard showcases 19th-century silhouettes.

The owners of the samplers displayed in the family room opposite arranged the works on the floor before hanging them to be sure they would be pleased with the placement.

Desk Accessories

Antique boxes, which were once used to hold documents and other important items, are still useful desk accessories today. The dome-lidded box above, an early-19th-century piece from Pennsylvania, is decorated with painted floral designs and has a pierced-tin clasp. It is about ten inches high.

Accessories artfully placed on a favorite piece of furniture can call attention to the piece, as well as form an attractive display in themselves. The owners of these two antique desks have made each a focal point with careful arrangements of objects.

The country secretary opposite, a "marriage" of a cupboard top and a blanket chest (a craftsman added the small drawers), is used to show off old leather-bound books, a wooden inkwell with quill pens, and an early-20th-century ship model with painted pressed-brass sails. The leather purse dates from around the turn of the 19th century.

In the parlor above, a Chippendale desk, still bearing its original red paint, provides a setting for books, glass and pewter inkwells, and a pair of 19th-century spectacles. An electrified redware jug, an 18th-century rushlight, and a reproduction sconce are part of the homeowner's extensive collection of antique and period-style lighting fixtures.

The stack of pantry boxes on the floor, opposite, and the painted storage boxes beside the desk, above, add to the "still life" effect of these two desk arrangements.

Small carved works are
charming additions to almost
any country setting. The
painted woodcarving of a
mother cat and her kitten,
above, was made by a
contemporary folk sculptor
from Pennsylvania. It is
about twelve inches long,
and the kitten is
detachable.

Thematic Accents

I n these three rooms, accessories have been grouped by theme, a good way to give the objects greater presence. The simple arrangement on the cupboard opposite includes two small dogs—one an 1800s brass nutcracker, the other a primitive toy whittled from an old box. Both appear to be admiring the oil portrait of a dog above them.

Nature sets the theme for the colorful grouping above left. Set on a blanket chest are a flower-painted tin document box and Victorian pincushions shaped like fruits and vegetables. On the wall are early-1800s theorem paintings, still lifes named for the stencils—or "theorems"—often used to make them.

The story of Adam and Eve, a favorite biblical subject among folk artists, was the inspiration for the display above right. The wood sculpture is a contemporary American piece; the reverse painting on glass is by the homeowner.

Fruits, flowers, and vegetables unify the display of theorem paintings, a painted tin box, and velvet pincushions, above left. The wood sculpture and the painting on glass, above right, depict Adam and Eve.

The animal grouping opposite includes an oil painting of a dog and a scherenschnitte *(or paper cutout) of horses on the walls, and two dogs on the 19th-century cupboard.*

141

FRAMED FOR DISPLAY

When considering accessories for your walls, you don't have to limit yourself to the obvious. Framed for display, humble household objects, or small mementos that might otherwise lie ignored in shoe boxes, can become imaginative decorations.

You might frame a single object, like an antique fan or a fragment of an old quilt, or try grouping small objects such as buttons, fishing flies, belt buckles, or vintage labels or bottle caps for a surprising display.

The success of your framed pieces will depend in part on the way they are arranged and mounted. Buttons can be grouped into a fanciful cluster of "grapes," a dainty embroidered handkerchief may be shown off against a darker background, or seed packets can be set into individual "compartments."

You will want to mount your items securely on a mat or a fabric background, using sewing thread, fine fishing line, or double-sided framer's tape. If you are concerned about damaging a valuable piece by framing it, take it to a professional, who can advise you on techniques for both mounting and framing.

The appealing colors, patterns, and shapes of a collection of bandboxes enliven the large, open stair landing above. Here the boxes mix well with other country accessories: a 19th-century jacquard coverlet and hooked rug, and a papier-mâché dog made around 1900.

Intriguing reminders of another time, bandboxes are popular country collectibles. While the containers were originally functional —the paper-covered boxes served as storage and as cheap, lightweight luggage—their rich colors and varied shapes now make them handsome decorative accessories.

Bandboxes originated in England in the 1600s as handy receptacles for the men's collarbands then in fashion—hence the name. The first examples were made of thin pieces of wood, but by the 1700s, pasteboard, a less expensive material, had become favored. In America, bandboxes were widely used by both men and women from about 1820 to 1850 to store and transport all manner of personal belongings.

By the early 1800s, the boxes also served another purpose: wallpaper manufacturers had taken to advertising their wares by wrapping bandboxes with their papers, and soon the companies were producing patterns specifically for the boxes. Common subjects included flowers, animals, mythology, and political events; views of coaches, sailing ships, and the new locomotives were designed to appeal to travelers.

Because the sizes and shapes of bandboxes vary considerably, ranging from large ovals to small hearts, the boxes lend themselves particularly well to being stacked, as on the landing of the 19th-century house above. These antique pieces date from the 1860s and 1870s.

The bandboxes opposite are part of another collection, assembled over the past twenty-five years. The fanciful display on the painted Pennsylvania corner shelf includes antiques, as well as new pieces that were handmade from cardboard and reproduction wallpapers. The boxes on the floor and stool all date from the 1800s.

Pretty Bandboxes

Because bandboxes come in so many shapes and sizes, they are ideal for decorating corners and other awkward spaces. On the corner shelf at left, small boxes make an interesting composition of colorful patterns. Larger boxes fill the space beneath.

Unexpected Touches

Accessories can be especially effective when used creatively in unexpected places. In the bathroom at left, for example, a collection of waterfowl decoys and bird carvings looks right at home. Continuing the "water" theme, the homeowners placed cast-iron frog doorstops along the wall behind the tub.

In a workroom, above, the simple look of redware milk pans and jugs and hand-blown glass bottles is particularly well suited to the austere space. A clutch of 19th-century powder horns is an appropriate addition.

Even a workroom like the one above, where old bottles sparkle on a sunny windowsill, is a place for accessories.

A bait sign is among the "aquatic" accessories that distinguish the bathroom at left.

147

Stairway Treatments

A painted stair runner, above left, imitates the color and pattern of an embroidered carpet. Cast-iron doorstops decorate the stairs above right.

An easy way to transform a staircase from a mere passageway into an attractive and unusual showcase is to decorate it with a judicious choice of accessories (carefully arranged for safety).

A striking runner, for example, adds pattern to the staircase above left. Crafted according to the traditional method for making floor cloths, this contemporary piece was made of heavy cotton duck, painted, and then varnished for protection. With its rich gold background and its stenciled vines of flowers, it provides a decorative focus against the teal-painted risers. The durable cloth not only holds up well under use, but also helps protect the steps beneath it.

On the steep 18th-century staircase above right, a collection of old doorstops is shown off to advantage against the black-and-white painted steps. "Door porters" like these cast-iron pieces were particularly popular between the late 1800s and the 1930s; they are typically shaped like animals or flower baskets, and are usually

bronzed or brightly painted. The examples shown here, each with its original paint, date from the early 20th century. Made in the same period, the rabbit sitting at the base of the stairs is a cast-iron lawn ornament.

The flight of stairs above left offers a good display space for a collection of 19th- and 20th-century baskets. The stained birch treads and white risers provide a simple backdrop for showing off the subtly varied shapes and textures of the pieces. Graduated in size from largest to smallest on each side of the stairs, the baskets lead the eye toward the landing, where a large cheese strainer set on a mid-19th-century hutch-table "caps" the arrangement.

Toys enliven the staircase above right. Facing in the same direction, the animals appear to lead the way upward and around the corner. The whimsical horses, nearly all of them wheeled pull toys from Germany, were made in the late 19th and early 20th centuries. The donkey by the newel post is a wind-up toy.

An "avenue" of baskets, including Appalachian and midwestern pieces, draws the eye up the staircase above left. Antique animals and an Ohio star quilt do the same on the stairs above right.

A
Lighthearted
Air

.· *The contemporary*
pincushion above was
modeled after the 19th-
century "sewing birds" that
clamped to worktables or
quilt frames to hold cloth in
place and to keep pins
handy. With its serpentine
design, this piece is an
intriguing decorative
accessory.

Whimsical accessories accentuate the lighthearted look established by the other furnishings in the bedroom at left, where the curved lines of the headboard on the unusual 19th-century cannon-ball bed are echoed by those of the wire-arm chandelier. Spool holders and a wind-up toy bird are displayed at the foot of the bed.

On the kitchen shelves above, humor can be found in the form of Pennsylvania German papier-mâché pip-squeaks: when a leather bellows in their base is squeezed, the toys squeak.

A whimsically shaped 1830s bed sets the tone for the cheerful accessories in the bedroom at left.

The humorous papier-mâché pip-squeak toys above, made in Pennsylvania between the late 1800s and the 1920s, include a rooster that emerges from his cage when the door is opened.

ANTIQUE DOORKNOBS

Antique doorknobs are details that give an authentic finish to an old house or a dash of charm to a new one. They can be found in diverse materials, including wood, iron, brass, bronze, copper, silver, ceramic, glass, and ivory. Doorknobs also vary considerably in their shape, size, and degree of decoration, reflecting the architectural styles in vogue when particular knobs were made.

Few doorknobs that exist today predate the early 1800s, when they began to be widely used in place of latches. In the 1820s, pressed glass was invented in America, and many knobs of that period were made from this material. From the 1870s to the 1890s, intricately decorated brass or bronze knobs became popular. Even then, different kinds of doorknobs were often used in the same house. Fancy ones were shown off in formal rooms such as the parlor, while plainer, less costly examples were used elsewhere.

Today, antique doorknobs are available from salvage and antique dealers specializing in architectural hardware and most can be adapted to a modern door. Reproductions can also be purchased.

The diversity of antique doorknobs is demonstrated by the colorful array at right. The clear, pressed-glass examples (upper left corner) were used as pulls on furniture and doors in the 1830s.

Wrought-iron hardware used on the closet doors above contrasts with the yellow paint. In the 18th and 19th centuries, hinges and latches were usually painted the same color as the woodwork.

Although door and cabinet hardware is primarily functional, such details as hinges, latches, locks, doorknobs, and drawer pulls can be decorative, enhancing the look of fine woodwork or accenting the particular style or period of a decor. In these two rooms, the hardware recalls the distinctive design and craftsmanship of early American wrought-iron pieces.

In the dressing room above, reproduction 18th-century-style strap hinges, and door pulls with spade-shaped cusps (or fastening ends), add interest to the pine doors and stand out well against the background of mustard yellow paint. The economical lines and understated design of Shaker cabinetry were the inspiration for the plain built-in drawers and closets that line the wall.

The simple wrought-iron thumb latches and H-L hinges chosen for the paneled doors in the bedroom opposite are reproductions of 19th-century hardware types. The H-L hinge, used widely until around the 1860s, began to replace the strap hinge at the beginning of the century.

With their simple, clean silhouettes, handwrought H-L hinges add interesting detail to the paneled closet door in the bedroom opposite. Such hinges were considered an improvement upon strap hinges, which were not as sturdy.

Decorative Hardware

Above, an 18th-century hand-forged iron thumb latch is shown from the back (top) and from the front, with its heart- and heart-and-diamond-shaped cusps (bottom). Thought to have been made as a love token for a bride, it appropriately adorns a master bedroom door today.

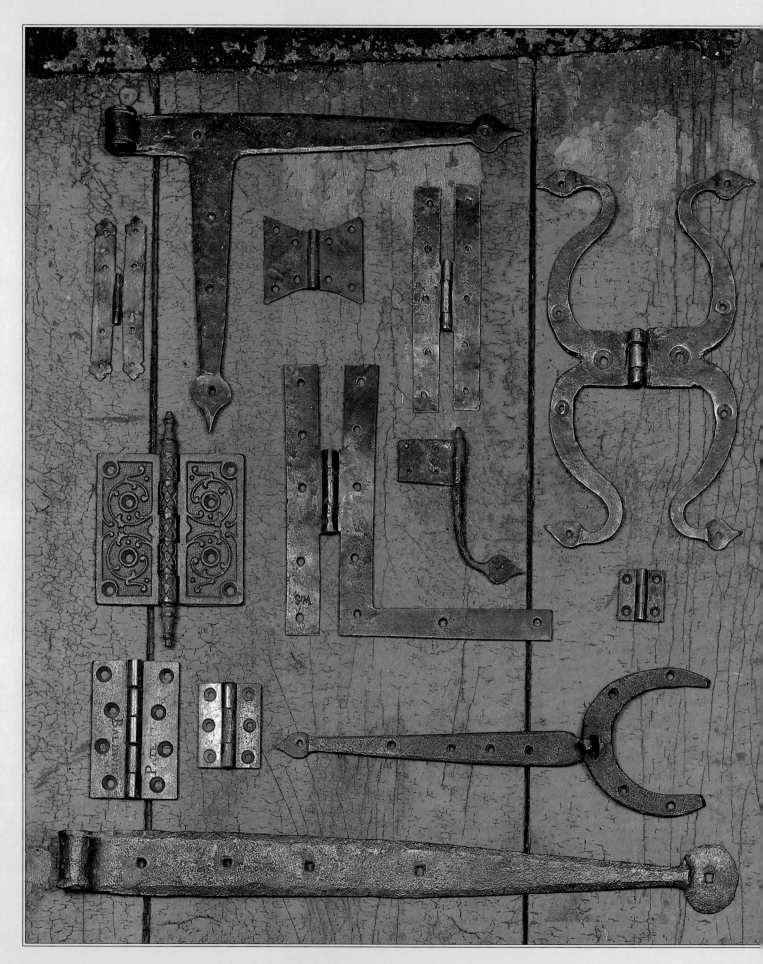

American Iron Hardware

Early American finish hardware —the visible hinges, latches, and handles used on doors, windows, cupboards, chests, and shutters— can be surprisingly beautiful. The cusps—or fastening ends—of latch handles were often worked into such shapes as hearts, spades, or pine trees. Hinges were often crafted into forms that inspired their names: "ram's horns," "ox shoes," "butterflies," and "rat tails."

Early American colonists at first imported their hardware from England, but as early as the 1700s German and English blacksmiths had set up forges in this country. Hand-wrought iron served most household purposes until the 1840s, when cast iron, which was less expensive to manufacture, became common.

Hardware styles were slow to change. Butterfly hinges as well as long strap hinges, for example, were used in the 1600s and 1700s. In the 1800s, large H and H-L hinges began to replace these earlier styles.

Today you can purchase period hardware from antique dealers and salvage specialists. New hardware can be custom-made to match antique pieces, and good stock reproductions are also available.

The 18th- and 19th-century latches and hinges at left are examples of the early wrought- and cast-iron hardware used in America. The pieces range from a hand-forged 1690 "foliated H" hinge, upper left, to an 1850s cast-iron latch, lower right.

Atop the grain-painted desk above is a rushlight, an early lighting device that usually held a rush wick dipped in tallow. Today, for convenience, it has been fitted with a homemade taper.

Traditional early American candle fixtures enhance the country look of this dining room, where antiques, as well as pieces handcrafted by the homeowner, are an important part of the decor.

The electrified tin chandelier at right, carefully made so that no wires are visible, is the main light source in the room. An early-19th-century candelabra on the table, a double-candle sconce, and hogscraper candlesticks provide accent lighting. In another part of the room, above, two 19th-century candle lanterns rest on the floor by an 1830s schoolmaster's desk. The tin sconce dates from the 1800s.

The hand-dipped candles in the dining room, right, are in keeping with the traditional light fixtures.

Traditional Lighting

The shield shape of the backplate on the antique candle sconce above indicates that the fixture was probably made in the early 1800s during the Federal period. The sconce is made of tin and the decoration is painted.

159

Creative Lighting

Lighting fixtures made from recycled materials can capture a period look and are interesting accents in any room. The chandelier in the bedroom at left, for example, was crafted from the leg of a damaged Federal-style table. An old chain and salvaged metal stripping, together with muffin tins for candle holders, were added to complete the unusual fixture, which was made by the homeowner. Its rustic look is a good complement to the other furnishings in the room, including the smoke-grained bed and the small chest at its foot, both New England pieces that date from the mid-1800s.

The lamp on the 19th-century painted tavern table above was made from an antique tin candle mold. The fabric shade was chosen to suit the simple base.

The chandelier at left is one of eight the homeowner made from the legs of an old table. An antique candle mold and a new, store-bought shade were combined to create the original table lamp above.

COUNTRY TABLE LAMPS

When well chosen, a table lamp can add a great deal of charm to a country room. Finding just the right country-style lamp is often difficult, however, so you might consider making a lamp yourself that works well with your decor. If you happen to be putting up wallpaper, why not use a piece to make a matching lampshade? If you have a collection of stoneware, try adapting a crock or a jug as a lamp base.

Indeed, objects as diverse as jars and candlesticks, kettles and toy blocks, can easily be turned into lamp bases. If you don't want to drill a wiring hole in an antique, you can use a special socket that allows the cord to come out the side.

Once you have chosen a base, give some thought to the shade, which is equally important. Generally, the depth of the shade should be about two inches less than the height of the base. A plain shade is best for a complicated or patterned base.

Among the handmade shades shown here are one with pressed flowers and one crafted from candlewicked muslin. The canning jar and brass candlestick lamps both have cut-and-pierced paper shades; the stoneware crock and jug have stenciled shades. Books on wiring lamps and on making shades can be purchased at craft supply stores.

Fireside Accessories

Accessories help make the fireplace the focal point in each of these country rooms. The owner of the early-19th-century Michigan house at left used antique household utensils, including candle molds and 19th-century cooking tools, to decorate her keeping room hearth. Cranberry swags and a Civil War-era training rifle hang from the mantel and complement the traditional look.

In the log cabin above, southwestern American Indian pottery, an Indonesian-made horse, and a Guatemalan folk-art carving used as a "fire screen" create an exotic mood at the hearth. The colorful objects are part of a collection of international pottery and folk art displayed throughout the house.

Baskets and dried herbs complement a traditional arrangement of hearth accessories at left.

The unusual accessories above have international folk origins: the horse is Indonesian; the carved feline, Guatemalan; and the turquoise-studded gourd and the ceramics were made by southwestern American Indians.

Focus on the Mantel

Redware jugs and an antique checkerboard give the mantel above left an early American look. Red candles accent the striking color scheme of the mantel arrangement above right.

Because the fireplace is often the focal point of a room, the mantel frequently becomes a convenient "shelf" for displays of small objects.

The handsome mantel arrangement in the 19th-century dining room above left draws its visual impact from the use of one type of object—redware jugs, set here side by side in graduated sizes (the miniatures were probably made as toys or souvenirs). Placing the jugs in this manner creates a simple but striking effect.

A basket hung on a crane lends interest to the fireplace opening.

On the mantel above right, a strong, basic color scheme—black and white accented with touches of deep red—calls attention to the display: against the off-white walls and white fireplace, decoys, candle molds and holders, and an early-20th-century hooked rug stand out in bold relief. Accessories around the hearth include an antique kettle made of cast iron and a 19th-century foot warmer.

An arrangement of objects related by a common color distinguishes the 18th-century mantel in the parlor above left. The pumpkin color of the paint on the mantelpiece and surrounding woodwork is picked up by a quartet of framed artworks: a 1784 love token—an early version of today's valentine—decorated with hearts, initials, and a sea serpent; a watercolor theorem painting in its original frame; an embroidered family record dated 1830; and a small watercolor portrait.

The mantel above right is decorated with an eclectic group of accessories that enhance the warm, lived-in look of the room. A primitive portrait forms the centerpiece of the arrangement, which includes pewter chargers and plates, heart-shaped molds, tin candlesticks, and toy sheep. Under the mantel hang handmade stockings and a flintlock rifle. A painted fireboard (a contemporary folk-art piece) and an old doll seated in a child's chair provide colorful accents on the hearth.

The staggered height of the artwork above left adds interest to the simple mantel. Pewter plates, above right, contribute to a seemingly unstudied arrangement.

Selected Reading

Birren, Faber. *Creative Color*. West Chester, Pa.: Schiffer Publishing, 1987.

Bishop, Adele, and Cile Lord. *The Art of Decorative Stenciling*. New York: Penguin Books, 1976.

Bogdonoff, Nancy Dick. *Handwoven Textiles of Early New England: The Legacy of a Rural People, 1640-1880*. Harrisburg, Pa.: Stackpole Books, 1975.

Boyce, Charles. *Dictionary of Furniture*. New York: Facts on File Publications, 1985.

Brittain, Judy, ed. *Terence Conran's Home Furnishings*. Boston: Little, Brown & Company, 1986.

Busch, Akiko. *Floorworks: Bringing Rooms to Life with Surface Design and Decoration*. Toronto: Bantam Books, 1988.

Comstock, Helen, ed. *The Concise Encyclopedia of American Antiques*. New York: Hawthorn Books, n.d.

Conran, Terence. *The House Book*. New York: Crown Publishers, 1982.

Cooke, Edward S., Jr., ed. *Upholstery in America from the Seventeenth Century to World War I*. New York: W.W. Norton & Company, 1987.

Dittrick, Mark, and Diane Kender Dittrick. *Decorative Hardware*. New York: Hearst Books, 1982.

Eastwood, Maud. *Antique Builders' Hardware: Knobs and Accessories*. Beaverton, Oreg.: Lithtex Printing, 1982.

Eastwood, Maud. *The Antique Doorknob*. Forest Grove, Oreg.: Times Litho, 1976.

Fernandez, Genevieve. *American Traditional: A Comprehensive Guide to Home Decorating the Ethan Allen Way*. New York: Simon and Schuster, 1984.

Fleming, John, Hugh Honour, and Nikolaus Pevsner. *The Penguin Dictionary of Architecture*. New York: Penguin Books, 1966.

Gilliatt, Mary. *Decorating: A Realistic Guide*. New York: Pantheon Books, 1977.

Gilliatt, Mary. *The Complete Book of Home Design*. Boston: Little, Brown & Company, 1984.

Grafton, Carol Belanger. *Victorian Cut and Use Stencils*. New York: Dover Publications, 1976.

Gray, Linda, with Jocasta Innes. *The Complete Book of Decorating Techniques*. Boston: Little, Brown & Company, 1986.

Grow, Lawrence. *Architectural Painting*. New York: Rizzoli, 1986.

Hague, William E., ed. *The Complete Basic Book of Home Decorating*. Garden City, N.Y.: Doubleday & Company, 1968.

Harris, Cyril M., ed. *Illustrated Dictionary of Historic Architecture*. New York: Dover Publications, 1977.

Hornung, Clarence P. *Treasury of American Design: A Pictorial Survey of Popular Folk Arts*. New York: Harry N. Abrams, 1971.

Houlihan, Patrick, Jerold L. Collings, Sarah Nestor, and Jonathan Batkin. *Harmony by Hand: Art of the Southwest Indians*. San Francisco: Chronicle Books, 1987.

Innes, Jocasta. *Paint Magic*. New York: Pantheon Books, 1981.

Kendrick, A.F., and C.E.C. Tattersall. *Hand-Woven Carpets: Oriental and European*. New York: Dover Publications, 1973.

Kopp, Joel, and Kate Kopp. *American Hooked and Sewn Rugs: Folk Art Underfoot*. New York: E.P. Dutton, 1985.

Le Grice, Lyn. *The Art of Stencilling*. New York: Clarkson N. Potter, 1986.

Lipman, Jean, and Tom Armstrong, eds. *American Folk Painters of Three Centuries*. New York: Hudson Hills Press, 1980.

Lipman, Jean, and Alice Winchester. *The Flowering of American Folk Art, 1776-1876*. New York: Viking Press, 1974.

Lott, Jane. *The Conran Home Decorator: Floors and Flooring*. New York: Villard Books, 1986.

Lynn, Catherine. *Wallpaper in America from the Seventeenth Century to World War I*. New York: W.W. Norton & Company, 1980.

Mayhew, Edgar deN., and Minor Myers, Jr. *A Documentary History of American Interiors from the Colonial Era to 1915*. New York: Charles Scribner's Sons, 1980.

Miller, Judith, and Martin Miller. *Period Details: A Sourcebook for House Restoration*. New York: Crown Publishers, 1987.

Montgomery, Florence M. *Textiles in America, 1650-1870*. New York: W.W. Norton & Company, 1984.

Niesewand, Nonie. *The Home Style Book*. New York: Whitney Library of Design, 1984.

Nylander, Richard C. *Wallpapers for Historic Buildings: A Guide to Selecting Reproduction Wallpapers*. Washington, D.C.: Preservation Press, 1983.

Nylander, Richard C., Elizabeth Redmond, and Penny J. Sander. *Wallpaper in New England*. Boston: Society for the Preservation of New England Antiquities, 1986.

O'Neil, Isabel. *The Art of the Painted Finish for Furniture and Decoration*. New York: William Morrow & Company, 1971.

Pettit, Florence H. *America's Printed and Painted Fabrics 1600-1900*. New York: Hastings House, 1970.

Pile, John F. *Interior Design*. New York: Harry N. Abrams, 1988.

Schiffer, Herbert, Peter Schiffer, and Nancy Schiffer. *Antique Iron: Survey of American and English Forms, Fifteenth through Nineteenth Centuries*. Exton, Pa.: Schiffer Publishing, 1979.

Seale, William. *Recreating the Historic House Interior*. Nashville: American Association for State and Local History, 1979.

Slayton, Mariette Paine. *Early American Decorating Techniques: Step-by-Step Directions for Mastering Traditional Crafts*. New York: Macmillan Company, 1972.

Smith, Carter. *Decorating with Americana: How to Know It, Where to Find It, and How to Make It Work for You*. Birmingham, Ala.: Oxmoor House, 1985.

Sprigg, June. *Shaker Design*. New York: W.W. Norton & Company, 1986.

Sudjic, Deyan, ed. *The House Style Book*. New York: Holt, Rinehart & Winston, 1984.

Waring, Janet. *Early American Stencils on Walls and Furniture*. New York: Dover Publications, 1968.

Weissman, Judith Reiter, and Wendy Lavitt. *Labors of Love: America's Textiles and Needlework, 1650-1930*. New York: Alfred A. Knopf, 1987.

Wilson, José, and Arthur Leaman. *Decorating American Style*. Boston: New York Graphic Society, 1975.

Wilson, Kax. *A History of Textiles*. Boulder, Colo.: Westview Press, 1979.

Photography Credits

Cover, frontispiece and pages 13, 20-21, 34-35, 40-43, 56, 59, 61, 64-65, 68-71, 76, 78, 81 (left), 86-87, 94-95, 104, 115, 128, 130, 136-137, 139 (right), 140-141 (except 140 left), 144-148, 151, 160, 164, 166 (left), 167 (left): George Ross. Pages 8-11, 18, 26-29, 36-37, 50, 81 (right), 84, 90-91, 97, 101, 102, 106-107, 112, 114, 116, 131, 138, 149, 155 (right), 156-157, 159 (right), 166 (right): Jon Elliott. Pages 12, 154-155 (except 155 right): Bradley Olman. Pages 14-15, 73: Bill Stites. Pages 16-17, 24-25, 44-47, 52-53, 60, 66-67, 82, 92-93, 96, 98, 108-109, 117-121, 126-127, 132-133, 142-143, 152-153, 162-163: Steven Mays. Pages 19, 72: David Frazier/*Home* Magazine. Pages 22-23, 51: Keith Scott Morton/*Decorating Remodeling* Magazine. Pages 30-31, 129: William Waldron. Pages 38-39, 110-111: Felice Frankel. Page 48: Ted Hardin. Page 49: Will Faller. Page 54: Stephen Donelian. Page 55: Tom Brenner. Page 57: Tom Yee/*Home* Magazine. Pages 58, 74-75: Richard Jeffery. Page 79: Richard Jeffery/*Home* Magazine. Pages 62-63: David Phelps. Page 80: Lizzie Himmel/*Home* Magazine. Pages 83, 122, 124-125: Phillip H. Ennis. Pages 85, 89, 113: Karen Bussolini. Pages 88, 103, 123, 134, 139 (left), 150 (right), 158-159 (except 159 right), 161, 165: Michael Luppino. Page 100: Robert Perron. Page 140 (left): Laurie Black/ARX. Page 150 (left): Brian Buckley. Page 167 (right): Lilo Raymond. Pages 118-121: illustrations by William J. Meyerriecks.

Prop Credits

The Editors would like to thank the following for their courtesy in lending items for photography. Items not listed below are privately owned. **Cover**: design consultant—Nancy Kalin, North Canton, OH. **Pages 10-11**: designed by Audrey Jackson, Welch, MN. **Page 12**: designed by Riki Gail Interiors, NYC. **Pages 16-17**: Selected wallcoverings and fabrics—Raintree Designs, NYC; China Seas, NYC; Motif Designs, New Rochelle, NY. Tiles—Country Floors, NYC. Decorative cord—M & J Trimming, NYC. Paint chips—Benjamin Moore Paints; Dutch Boy, Mark II. **Page 19**: designed by Scruggs & Myers, Salem, NC. **Page 21**: grain-painted boxes—Carroll Hopf, Kennebunk, ME. **Pages 24-25**: Top row: All-American theme: wallcoverings—"Blue Calico," "Red Gingham"—Gear, NYC; Pastels theme: wallcoverings—"Taylor Trellis," green, "Leslie Blue" on white; fabric—"Norma Yellow" on white—Hinson & Co., NYC; Stripes and fruits theme: wallcovering—"Lyme Regis," coral; fabric—"Orchard," multi duck egg—Laura Ashley Home Furnishings, NYC; Colonial theme: wallcoverings—"Quilt Star," rust on ivory, "Betsy Brown's Blanket," rust on ivory; fabric—"Slipware Stripe," ivory on rust—Hinson & Co. Bottom row: Coordinated florals theme: wallcoverings—"Jennifer," red on white, "Diana," red on white; fabric—"Tommy," blue on white—Hinson & Co. Traditional patterns theme: wallcoverings — "Cambridge," beige, "Cranston Plaid," red; fabric—"Country Fancy," indigo—Waverly Fabrics, NYC. Neutrals theme: wallcoverings—"Alexandra," white on sand, "Pinehurst," beige on white; fabric—"MacDougall White"—Hinson & Co; Paisley and foulard theme: wallcovering—"Hatfield Foulard"; fabric—"Brooke"—The Ralph Lauren Home Collection, NYC. **Pages 30-31**: lace and linen—paper white, ltd., Fairfax, CA; glass coffee table, painted wooden panel on mantel, and white porcelain fruit basket on coffee table—Pierre Deux, NYC; wool throw on chair—Treadles, NYC; candlesticks and straw basket—Pottery Barn, NYC; urn in left corner—Terrafirma, NYC; stripped pine day bed and settee—Evergreen Antiques, NYC. **Pages 34-35**: designed by Ronald Bricke of Ronald Bricke & Associates, NYC, with thanks to Decorator Previews, NYC. **Pages 42-43**: designed by Ronald Bricke of Ronald Bricke & Associates, NYC, with thanks to Decorator Previews, NYC. **Pages 44-45**: designed by Anita Walker, Ponchatoula, LA. **Page 50**: all furniture from Pickering Place & Partners Antiek, Lionville, PA. **Pages 52-53**: see wallpaper schematic, page 171: (1) "Otis Garland Border," Society for the Preservation of New England Antiquities, reproduction — Brunschwig & Fils, NYC; (2) "Star Border," Williamsburg adaptation—Katzenbach & Warren, NYC; (3) "Mistletoe Border," Williamsburg adaptation—Katzenbach & Warren; (4) "Portsmouth Pineapple," Williamsburg adaptation—Katzenbach & Warren; (5) "Clarissa Festoon Borders," SPNEA adaptation—Brunschwig & Fils; (6) "Williamsburg Vineyard," Williamsburg adaptation—Katzenbach & Warren; (7) "Stencil Flowers," Williamsburg adaptation—Katzenbach & Warren; (8) "Plymouth Stencil," reproduction—Waterhouse Wallhangings Inc., Boston; (9) "Louise," reproduction—Waterhouse Wallhangings Inc.; (10) "Williamsburg Apples," Williamsburg adaptation—Katzenbach & Warren; (11) "Beacon Hill Diamond," SPNEA adaptation—Brunschwig & Fils; (12) "Bulfinch Swag and Border," SPNEA reproduction—Brunschwig & Fils; (13) "Brodsworth," adaptation—Waterhouse Wallhangings Inc.; (14) "Leaf Stripe," Williamsburg adaptation—Katzenbach & Warren; (15) "Otis Damask," SPNEA reproduction—Brunschwig & Fils; (16) "Carolina Toile," Williamsburg adaptation—Katzenbach & Warren; (17) "Thayer Blossom," SPNEA reproduction—Brunschwig & Fils; (18) "Dorset,"

Williamsburg reproduction—Katzenbach & Warren; (19) "Woodbury Moiré," SPNEA reproduction—Brunschwig & Fils; (20) "Cornflower Resist," SPNEA reproduction—Brunschwig & Fils; (21) "Wheat Damask," reproduction—Waterhouse Wallhangings Inc. **Page 54**: hardwood moldings—National Moulding and Ornament Ltd., Glen Head, NY; Nomastyl moldings (made of dense polystyrene)—NMC Decorations, Zebulon, NC. **Page 56**: stenciled by Beth Criger, Royal Oak, MI. **Page 57**: designed by Lynn Goodpasture, NYC, for Mary Zick Interiors, Greenwich, CT; stenciled by Lynn Goodpasture. **Page 59**: painted and stenciled by Wiggins Brothers, Tilton, NH. **Pages 60-61**: "Lang Vine" pattern created and stenciled by Lynn Goodpasture, NYC, ©1980. **Pages 64-65**: painted by Wiggins Brothers, Tilton, NH. **Pages 66-67**: ragged wall created by Fred Smith, Brooklyn, NY; antique pine chest—Evergreen Antiques, NYC. **Page 72**: designed by Scruggs & Myers, Salem, NC. **Page 83**: designed by Ronald Bricke of Ronald Bricke & Associates, NYC, with thanks to Decorator Previews, NYC. **Pages 86-87**: floor cloths—Good & Co. Floorclothmakers, Amherst, NH. **Pages 90-91**: designed by Audrey Jackson, Welch, MN. **Pages 92-93**: antique rag rugs—Victor Weinblatt, antique rug dealer, South Hadley, MA. **Page 96**: designed by Anita Walker, Ponchatoula, LA. **Page 97**: designed by Audrey Jackson, Welch, MN. **Page 98**: strip flooring: "Williamsburg Strip," natural red oak—Chickasaw Hardwood Floors, Memphis, TN; plank flooring: "Heritage Plank," pegged oak, antique finish—Chickasaw Hardwood Floors; parquet flooring: Wood Flor-Tile, solid oak, honey—Hartco/Tibbals Flooring Co., Oneida, TN. **Page 103**: designed by Mary Meehan Interiors, NYC. **Page 104**: designed by Renée Leonard, NYC; antiques and accessories—Eggs & Tricity, NYC; chintz quilt on chaise and star quilt on rack—Judith and James Milne, Inc., NYC. **Pages 108-109**: calicoes courtesy of: Cheryl Mackley, Delta, PA; Susan Parrish Antiques, NYC; Bill Span, The Packrats, Silver Spring, MD; Margaret Canavan, Silver Spring, MD. **Pages 112-113**: design consultant—Nancy Kalin, North Canton, OH. **Page 117**: designed by Anita Walker, Ponchatoula, LA. **Page 118**: "Adelaide" fabric—The Ralph Lauren Home Collection, NYC. **Page 119**: "Club Check" fabric—Laura Ashley Home Furnishings, NYC. **Page 120**: "Granite Stripe" fabric, blueberry—Gear, NYC. **Page 121**: "Mr. Georgie's Grid" fabric—The Tilling Collection, Raintree Designs, NYC. **Page 122**: designed by Ronald Bricke of Ronald Bricke & Associates, NYC, with thanks to Decorator Previews, NYC. **Page 123**: designed by Mary Meehan Interiors, NYC. **Pages 124-125**: designed by Ronald Bricke of Ronald Bricke & Associates, NYC, with thanks to Decorator Previews, NYC. **Page 128**: designed by Madeline Armeson, Dennisport, MA. **Page 129**: all bed linens—paper white, ltd., Fairfax, CA. **Page 130**: stenciled by Beth Criger, Royal Oak, MI. **Page 131**: design consultant—Nancy Kalin, North Canton, OH. **Pages 132-133**: American Indian blankets, antique chair—Kelter/Malcé Antiques, NYC. **Page 138**: designed by Audrey Jackson, Welch, MN. **Pages 142-143**: mantel—Danny Alessandro, NYC; framed glass and Bakelite buttons, silver and scrimshaw pieces—Tender Buttons, NYC; antique lace pieces and handkerchief—Trouvaille Française, NYC; all other pieces—Park Slope Framing/Phyllis Wrynn, Brooklyn, NY. **Page 148**: floor cloth on staircase—Good & Co. Floorclothmakers, Amherst, NH. **Page 151**: stenciled by Beth Criger, Royal Oak, MI. **Pages 152-153**: antique doorknobs and pulls—M.L. Eastwood, antique doorknob consultant, Tillamook, OR. **Pages 154-155**: designed by Riki Gail Interiors, NYC. **Pages 156-157**: antique hinges and latches—Monroe Coldren & Sons Antiques, West Chester, PA. **Pages 162-163**: lampshades and bases designed and created by Judy Tripp, Mainely Shades, Falmouth, ME.

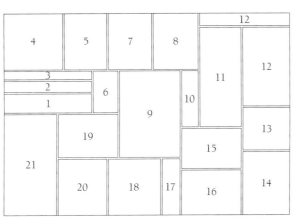

Schematic for wallpapers appearing on pages 52 and 53. All patterns are shown approximately one-tenth actual size.

Index

Acknowledgments

Our thanks to Madeline Armeson, Judy and Alex Awrylo, Don Bollinger, Katharine and Robert E. Booth, Jr., Duane and Mary Margaret Boyd, Ronald Bricke, Mason and Frank Brower, Nancy Cayford, Bette and David Chenault, Michael Coldren, Jimmy Cramer, Barbara and Player Crosby, Jeannine and Otto Dobbs, Ola Flick, Riki Gail, Lynn Goodpasture, Edward and Sheri Grossman, Margaret and Charles Gure, Claudia and Carroll Hopf, Audrey and Mark Jackson, Dean Johnson, Richard and Janet Lang, Renée Leonard, William Lewan, Kenneth Martin, Mary Meehan, National Paint & Coatings Association, National Wood Flooring Association, Barbara and Charles Randau, Nancy Clark Reynolds, Marilyn Simmons, Claude Taylor, Michaele Thunen, Anita and Johnny Walker, Holly and David Wesley, Kathy and Ken Wilson, Eileen and Carter Wiseman, Phyllis Wrynn, and Mary and John Zick for their help on this book.

Third printing
Published simultaneously in Canada
School and library distribution by Silver Burdett Company,
Morristown, New Jersey

TIME-LIFE is a trademark of Time Incorporated U.S.A.

Production by Giga Communications, Inc.
Printed in U.S.A.

Library of Congress Cataloging-in-Publication Data

Country decorating
p.cm.—(American country)
Includes index.
ISBN 0-8094-6758-5. ISBN 0-8094-6759-3 (lib. bdg.)
1. Decoration and ornament, Rustic—United States—History—
20th century. 2. Interior decoration—United States—History—
20th century. I. Time-Life Books. II. Series.
NK2002.C58 1988
747.213—dc19 88-24771
CIP

American Country was created by Rebus, Inc., and published by Time-Life Books.

REBUS, INC.

Publisher: RODNEY FRIEDMAN • Editor: MARYA DALRYMPLE
Senior Editor: RACHEL D. CARLEY • Managing Editor: BRENDA SAVARD • Consulting Editor: CHARLES L. MEE, JR.
Associate Editor: SARA COLLINS MEDINA • Writers: JUDITH CRESSY, ROSEMARY G. RENNICKE
Freelance Writers: DON BOLLINGER, JOE L. ROSSON, MARY SEARS
Design Editors: NANCY MERNIT, CATHRYN SCHWING
Test Kitchen Director: GRACE YOUNG • Editor, The Country Letter: BONNIE J. SLOTNICK
Editorial Assistants: SANTHA CASSELL, CAROLE McCURDY • Contributing Editors: ANNE MOFFAT,
DEE SHAPIRO • Indexer: IAN TUCKER

Art Director: JUDITH HENRY • Associate Art Director: SARA REYNOLDS
Designer: SARA BOWMAN • Assistant Designer: TIMOTHY JEFFS
Photographer: STEVEN MAYS • Photo Editor: SUE ISRAEL
Photo Assistant: ROB WHITCOMB • Freelance Photographers: LAURIE BLACK,
STEPHEN DONELIAN, JON ELLIOTT, PHILLIP ENNIS, MICHAEL LUPPINO, BRADLEY OLMAN,
DAVID PHELPS, GEORGE ROSS, WILLIAM WALDRON • Freelance Photo Stylist: VALORIE FISHER

Consultants: BOB CAHN, HELAINE W. FENDELMAN,
LINDA C. FRANKLIN, GLORIA GALE, KATHLEEN EAGEN JOHNSON, ELEANOR LEVIE,
JUNE SPRIGG, CLAIRE WHITCOMB

Time-Life Books Inc. is a wholly owned subsidiary of TIME INCORPORATED.

FOUNDER: HENRY R. LUCE 1898-1967

Editor-in-Chief: JASON McMANUS • Chairman and Chief Executive Officer: J. RICHARD MUNRO
President and Chief Operating Officer: N. J. NICHOLAS JR. • Editorial Director: RAY CAVE
Executive Vice President, Books: KELSO F. SUTTON • Vice President, Books: GEORGE ARTANDI

TIME-LIFE BOOKS INC.

Editor: GEORGE CONSTABLE • Executive Editor: ELLEN PHILLIPS
Director of Design: LOUIS KLEIN • Director of Editorial Resources: PHYLLIS K. WISE
Editorial Board: RUSSELL B. ADAMS JR., DALE M. BROWN, ROBERTA CONLAN, THOMAS H. FLAHERTY,
LEE HASSIG, DONIA ANN STEELE, ROSALIND STUBENBERG
Director of Photography and Research: JOHN CONRAD WEISER
Assistant Director of Editorial Resources: ELISE RITTER GIBSON

President: CHRISTOPHER T. LINEN • Chief Operating Officer: JOHN M. FAHEY JR.
Senior Vice Presidents: ROBERT M. DeSENA, JAMES L. MERCER, PAUL R. STEWART
Vice Presidents: STEPHEN L. BAIR, RALPH J. CUOMO, NEAL GOFF, STEPHEN L. GOLDSTEIN,
JUANITA T. JAMES, HALLETT JOHNSON III, CAROL KAPLAN, SUSAN J. MARUYAMA,
ROBERT H. SMITH, JOSEPH J. WARD
Director of Production Services: ROBERT J. PASSANTINO

For information about any Time-Life book please call 1-800-621-7026, or write:
Reader Information, Time-Life Customer Service
P.O. Box C-32068, Richmond, Virginia 23261-2068

Time-Life Books Inc. offers a wide range of fine recordings, including a Rock 'n' Roll Era series.
For subscription information, call 1-800-621-7026, or write TIME-LIFE MUSIC,
P.O. Box C-32068, Richmond, Virginia 23261-2068.